Joseph C. McCutchen

$5\frac{35}{}$

Generation
to
Generation

GENERATION
to
GENERATION

Conversations on Religious Education and Culture

by John H. Westerhoff III
and Gwen Kennedy Neville

A Pilgrim Press Book
from
UNITED
CHURCH
PRESS

Philadelphia

Library of Congress Cataloging in Publication Data

Westerhoff, John H.
   Generation to generation; conversations on religious
education and culture.

   "A Pilgrim Press book."
   Includes bibliographical references.
   1. Religious education—Addresses, essays, lectures.
2. Religion and culture—Addresses, essays, lectures.
I. Neville, Gwen Kennedy, 1938–   joint author.
II. Title.
BV1473.W47   200'.1   74–508
ISBN 0–8298–0274–6

   Excerpts on pages 34 and 46 are from *The Social Construction of Reality* by Peter L. Berger and Thomas Luckmann. Copyright © 1966 by Peter L. Berger and Thomas
Luckmann. Reprinted by permission of Doubleday & Company, Inc. Biblical quotations are from the *Revised Standard Version of the Bible,* copyright 1946 and 1952 by the
Division of Christian Education, National Council of
Churches, and are used by permission.

United Church Press, 1505 Race Street,
Philadelphia, Pennsylvania 19102

Dedicated to our teachers
and our students—
past, present, and future

CONTENTS

PREFACE

Conversations and Concerns

This book is a collection of essays, the offspring of the almost unexplored union of anthropology and religious education. Its content: a descriptive and analytical discussion of the interface between *religion* and *culture,* especially the dynamics of how both are transmitted from parent to child within religious-cultural communities. Its goal: to assist churches in discovering new forms for their educational ministry. Its audience: all those concerned for religious education.

The Why of This Book

We have specifically not aimed these essays at either the church or the seminary. In a day when so many of the fundamental decisions affecting local churches have become the exclusive domain of distant experts, we have undertaken the task of providing a resource that attempts to bridge the gap between professional and lay persons involved in religious education. We believe that in order for congregations and their leaders to make intelligent decisions they need easy access to the theories and insights of professional and academic scholars. We also believe that there is a need for these scholars to understand and communicate better with persons other than their colleagues. Our aim has been that of middle persons in these two endeavors.

Thus, in the formation of this book, we have had to face a number of quandaries. The first was the tension between writing a popular book and writing an academic treatise. Our decision was to steer between these alternatives, attempting to present sound, verifiable data from each of our disciplines while offering them in understandable and usable form. Another quandary involved a choice between writing together a unified, systematic work on culture and religious socialization and collecting a number of our individually written essays. We chose the latter, combining lectures and articles from the two-year period in which we have been conversing, criticizing, and learning from one another. The result is a merger of diverse material and comment by an anthropologist interested in religion and a religious educator interested in anthropology. We hope this approach provides an introduction to our two disciplines in conversation, a growing need amid the explosion of knowledge and resulting specialization.

The essays included were written for various occasions. Each might have grown into a book. Some repeat concerns or thoughts found in others. None is written to our total satisfaction. We chose large issues and handled them in an introductory fashion. Deciding that it was important for these issues and questions to be raised and discussed now, we chose not to wait until we had formulated fully defensible and footnoted positions or a single thesis.

We therefore envision this book primarily as an educational resource for individuals and groups concerned about religious education, rather than an original academic contribution to either of our specific disciplines. Our desire is to apply some of the knowledge that is now stored in libraries and journals to practical questions facing educators in the church. Realizing that our content is far from exhaustive, we believe that there are new questions and fresh approaches waiting to be discussed and that the disciplines of anthropology and religious education, when combined, can provide a starting point for some of those conversations.

Who Are the Conversationists?

Two people from such diverse backgrounds writing a book on religious socialization precipitates the question of how we met, how our conversation began, and how we decided to write a book. This is the story: Gwen Neville is an anthropologist who teaches on the faculty of Emory University in Atlanta, Georgia. She holds the Ph.D. degree from the University of Florida, where her doctoral dissertation was on the Southern Presbyterians at Montreat, North Carolina. Having been raised in Texas, Gwen now lives in Atlanta with her husband and three children.

John Westerhoff is the editor of *Colloquy* magazine and a secretary for religious education in the United Church Board

13

for Homeland Ministries. He is completing his Ed.D. in religion and education at Teachers College, Columbia University, and will, in September 1974, join the faculty of Duke University Divinity School in Durham, North Carolina. He is an ordained minister in the United Church of Christ, is married, and has three children.

We, the protagonists, met in 1971 at a World Council of Churches conference on the world education crisis. Our conversations began around the problems of education and the role played by culture in learning. Discussions developed into a friendship that has grown through the years, including collaboration for a special issue of *Colloquy* and joint participation at workshops on religious education. Each has learned from the discipline of the other.

We share a common concern for human beings, for the world, and for the future of the church. We both read in the fields of education, religion, and anthropology; we have been active in the Council on Anthropology and Education as well as in church educational endeavors. This book is the first tangible product of our long hours of enriching conversations, many of which resulted in a chapter, as well as in an occasional argument. To tie these individual articles together, we each responded briefly to the other's essay. Perhaps that will help make this book a better study resource and will enlarge the circle of participants in our own continuing discussion.

The decisive impetus to put these essays together into a book came following an untimely accident. In March of 1973, John was in a car accident and fractured his neck, an injury requiring a long period of recuperation. This gave him both the impetus and the time to work. Gwen agreed to take the extra time from her busy schedule to cooperate in the endeavor. Of course, the project would never have come to fruition if it had not been for the help of John's secretary, Carmeta Krause, who put the manuscript in order; our editors, who prepared it for publication; our colleagues, who encouraged us; and, most of all, our families, who affirmed us as we took time away from them to write.

The Basic Order and Sequence

Section One, Groups, Group Life, and Religious Socialization, attempts to make some statements about the dynamics of communal life and religious communities in the education process.

"Protestants and Roman Catholics Together" is a product of conversations John has had with his friend, Fr. Mark Heath, now director of the Washington Theological Consortium in Washington, D.C.

"What Is Religious Socialization?" was originally written for a course at Union Theological Seminary and then later used as the basis for an experimental religious education program at Andover Newton Theological School; an earlier version appeared in the *Andover Newton Quarterly.*

Gwen's essay, "The Sacred Community—Kin and Congregation in the Transmission of Culture," is based upon her doctoral dissertation at the University of Florida. That dissertation should be available in book form soon.

"Religious Education for the Maypole Dancers" was first delivered as the Lentz Lecture on Education in the Church at Harvard Divinity School, where John taught during his 1973 sabbatical. That version was published in *Religious Education.* It has been revised and edited for this book.

The essay "Rites and Rituals for a Double World—Private and Public Meanings" grew out of a workshop that Gwen and John conducted in the spring of 1972. It was our first attempt to combine religious education and anthropology around a specific problem.

We have focused on the person and specific life phases in Section Two, The Individual and the Life Cycle in the Educational Process.

"The Faith of Children" resulted from John's conversations with a Harvard colleague, Jim Fowler, who is studying faith development. It is based upon research conducted by Ann Trevelyan, a doctoral student at Harvard who participated in John's course on religious socialization.

"The Learning of Values" John wrote for use in courses to be given at the American Church in Paris and at the Presbyterian Conference Center, Ghost Ranch, New Mexico, 1973.

A version of "Sex and Socialization" was delivered at Harvard by Gwen as a Lentz Lecturer on Women's Studies during 1972. It also appears in a new book edited by Alice Hageman entitled *Sexist Religion and Women in the Churches,* published by Association Press, 1974.

"Reshaping Adults" John wrote specifically for this collection.

It represents some of his last thoughts as we reflected on our conversations to date and the state of the church in American culture.

The essay "Continuity and Change in Human Culture" was published in the September 1971 issue of *Colloquy,* which was designed to introduce *Colloquy's* readers to anthropology and education.

For learning resources and references, we have included Section Three, Religion, Education, and Culture—Readings and Resources. "Anthropology of Religion" outlines Gwen's graduate seminar at Emory. "The Church As a Learning Community" outlines John's pro-seminar at Harvard on anthropology and religious education. We hope these will be of some help to those who want to use this book as a starting point for further study. Our footnotes are lengthy for the same reasons.

Now while this might normally close our introduction, we decided that a few more introductory comments were needed if our book was to be used profitably. Two things we felt it necessary to include: a few words about anthropology as a discipline and a few words about religious education today.

From the Anthropologist

The word anthropologist conjures up a vision of dense jungles and pith helmets, or perhaps one of hot sun-drenched deserts and tedious archaeological excavations. Even more recently the word been extended in the public mind to include Louis S. B. Leakey, noted African paleontologist, along with Margaret Mead for the primitives and Desmond Morris for the monkeys and apes. Very few people know of "the other anthropology," that arm of the discipline concerned with the social and cultural worlds of modern urban Americans.

Urban anthropology is one label used for those who apply the old ethnographic methods of field study and participant observation to the new context of city and town life in present-day communities. The title is a misnomer, however. There is not an "urban anthropology" any more than there is a "primitive anthropology" or a "rural anthropology."

The science of anthropology has always been concerned with a very broad range of societies and cultures at every level of complexity and from the beginning of time. This concern begins with a quest for the meaning of human culture and human society in all their fascinating variations. What constitutes "humanness" and sets us apart from our primate relatives? What effect does biology have on culture? How does environment limit and facilitate human cultural growth? What is the significance of symbolic language and how do we understand the structuring of separate realities through language? What are the factors in cultural difference? How do you account for cultural change over time?

All these questions occupy the social, or cultural, anthropologist in the search for regularities to explain our universe. In the past few decades the endeavors of some of these researchers have turned partially toward practical usage of the now-extensive museum vaults of scientific knowledge about humans and their groupings. Applied uses for cultural data have been found in planning overseas programs and in training individuals for cross-cultural jobs, in designing culturally sensitive curricula for urban ethnic schools, in executing more livable housing in redevelopment projects, and in delivering more efficient and usable health care to racial and cultural minorities. One brand of the new-style applied anthropology is specifically aimed at action programs and identifies with radical change, such as American Indian protest activity and that of other oppressed groups.

My own interest in anthropology grew out of a need to understand the process of change and the resistance to change that occurs within traditional U.S. subcultures. I first witnessed this resistance while attempting to be a change agent within the education program of a Protestant congregation in the South. Gradually, as I learned more about the social structure of the congregation, its cultural heritage and built-in world view and values, it became more apparent that the standardized religious education curriculum from the National Board was being rejected as surely and effectively as a Peruvian village rejects U.S. health practices. They were from outside the local cultural grooves and were *not* culturally sensitive!

I am eager to apply the knowledge of human cultural systems to the specific problems of education. It is a special challenge to attempt to bring this type of analysis into the realm of *religious* education.

If we are able to delineate and understand the grooves of

religious cultures within American life and to grasp the explicit dynamics of the cultural transmission process, we will have come far toward appreciating the beauty of the natural human universe. This appreciation is crucial in preserving the best of tradition while attempting to bring about constructive educational change.

From the Religious Educator

The search for a means to sustain and transmit the Christian faith is as old as the church itself. Yet in every age the challenge is addressed anew. Our book, like others before it, is a product of its time. That cannot be denied. At the same time it is a part of a long history. The concerns of the book are not new, nor probably even its thesis. In the future the same issue will need to be addressed afresh; it is good to remind oneself of that. At best this book is one in a long line of attempts to answer the question: What is religious education? Our hope is to make a contribution to that continually important dialogue. The search for the means to sustain and transmit the church's faith will continue. We hope that our insights, whether they prove true or false, will help in the continuing quest for knowledge.

In any case we, like all writers on religious education, have an implied theology and a methodological bias which has influenced our opinions. That's always been true.

During the twenties and thirties, at the height of the religious education movement, "liberalism" dominated main-line Protestant theology. Emphasizing the ethical dimension of Christianity, liberalism affirmed the infinite dignity and value of persons, persons who possessed unlimited potential for moral and spiritual growth. Religious education tended to mirror the theological scene. With a goal of moral and character development, and highly critical of those methods which tried to teach "religion," many religious educators, secure in a romantic view that children would "naturally" develop those beliefs and moral virtues necessary for a healthy society, affirmed a "free approach" to religious nurture.

Not too many years went by before historical situations brought change to the theological scene. The aims and methods of education changed correspondingly. With the birth of neo-orthodoxy a new concern for the transmission of beliefs emerged. The content of scripture became central to the teaching task as salvation replaced character development. The educational problem was now clearly a theological problem. Soon "Christian" education was to replace "religious" education as the proper concern of the church. The Presbyterian U.S.A. "Faith and Life" curriculum was demonstrative of these changes in the theological scene.

The story could go on. Existentialism made its contribution, and so did other theological positions. Today a theology of particularisms (black theology, liberation theology, hope theology, and so forth) is influencing what is now commonly called church education. Educators can neither ignore nor completely transcend the theology of their day. Perhaps we should never try. It does help, however, to be aware of the forces which influence us.

In like manner, religious educators need to realize that many other forces influence our activities. Take, for example, the social sciences. For a long time certain schools of psychology have dominated religious education. The depth psychologies of the forties and fifties were an obvious influence. Both the Seabury series and the United Church Curriculum show the effect some of the psychologically oriented pastoral theologians had in the days of their creation. But the social sciences also change. Today developmental psychology (the work of Piaget, Kohlberg, and others) has begun to emerge as a dominant influence on church education. Likewise, new curricula and understandings of teaching and learning are surfacing to correspond to the changes in general education. The United Church's new "Shalom Curriculum" is a good example of the merging of contemporary biblical theological conviction, social concerns, and educational methodology.

Following these historical shifts can help educators get a perspective on their latest enthusiasms. We make a number of errors simply because we are ignorant of our past. It might be helpful, therefore, to remember that in some periods nurture was emphasized and in others conversion; in some schooling and in others nonschooling; in some the individual and in others groups; in some children and in others adults; and in some education in the church and in others education in the public sector. It's been called religious education, Christian education, and church education. Over the years the emphases have been different within Roman Catholicism and Protestantism, on the Continent and in the States. The church's search for a Christian education continues.

Today it is difficult to know what is the dominant influence. We are in a period of transition. There is no dominant theology or, for that matter, dominant social science. We are perhaps more conscious of our failures in the recent past than we are sure of what we must do in the future. Diversity is the dominant mode of the times. In just such a period, dialogue and experimentation are of tremendous importance. A period of transition is a very exciting time because it makes possible new thoughts and new ideas. Change periods are periods when new thoughts and actions can emerge, while trend periods with their dominant theology or social science make it difficult for a new idea to surface.

There is, of course, an implied theology in this book. We may not ourselves be entirely aware of it, nor have we attempted to explicate it fully. Our choice of the words "intentional religious socialization" and "religious education to be Christian" are loaded with theological assumptions and implications. All we can say for sure is that John has been influenced by the "neo-liberal-liberation-hope theology" of our day. And, of course, our choice of the social science discipline of anthropology has influenced our understanding. We are aware that we have not drawn heavily on those of sociology or psychology. Both these views have made significant input to education in the church already. Now, we propose to add the approach from cultural anthropology, perhaps a fresh way of looking at our problem, of stating our questions, and of seeking our solutions. These contributions are offered as an addition to, not a replacement of, the others which are being made in our own time as the church continues its search for Christian education.

Finally, the phrase "religious socialization" is not intended as the new jargon word of the day. Neither is the term "cultural transmission." We're not eager to gain followers but instead to encourage a rethinking of old problems and to stimulate new questions, beyond our own. This is a first step for us. We fully expect to change and to rearrange our positions and opinions. We expect to learn from our critics as well as from our advocates. We only hope that you will join us in our conversation and in our search.

INTRODUCTION

by C. Ellis Nelson

Skinner and McAlpin Professor
of Practical Theology
Union Theological Seminary,
New York City

Warning: the book you are about to read may make you dizzy!

If you know how culture shapes your life, then you need no warning. You can proceed quickly through this manuscript, noting how the acculturation process is related to religious education.

If you are in the roughly 90 percent of the population who has not given serious thought to what culture is or how it affects every moment of your life, then you should read this introduction carefully to get some idea of what is in store for you. Don't feel that, because you are part of the 90 percent, your education was defective or that you are slow-witted. The idea of culture and what it does to form personality is exceedingly complex and goes down to the unconscious level of our being. Yes, even the content and interpretation of dreams is culture-bound. So to analyze culture is a tough proposition because it requires that we deal with vague but exceedingly powerful matters, such as what we think is "good" or "bad." And what we think is "good" or "bad" is so obvious to us and motivates our mind and body so spontaneously that we have trouble getting a hold on it long enough to think about it.

If we do get a hold on the notion of culture, another difficulty arises: We can't understand it without separating ourselves from it. That is, we must be able to exercise a certain amount of self-transcendence. We have to achieve the small miracle of imagining what we would be like if we had grown up as an American Indian or a member of the Masai tribe in Kenya. Until we are able to step out of our skin and feel what it is like to have a different environment, we are not able to understand the formative power of culture. Ralph Linton, professor of Anthropology at Columbia University, put it this way: "For a person to discover culture is like a fish discovering that he is living in water."

Discover is the right word. Culture is everywhere but is as un-thought-about as wearing clothes. Of course, in a general way, we know the Eskimos have customs and clothes strange to Americans. We identify and picture these differences just as the *National Geographic* does. We enjoy knowing about quaint customs or we react with revulsion to the descriptions of head-hunting cannibals. It is not until we begin to ask why we enjoy knowing about other people in the world or to wonder why we feel queasy in the stomach at the idea of eating human flesh that we begin to discover culture. And once we make the discovery, there is a tendency to go through three stages of awareness.

The first stage is the realization that a great deal of our life which we consider "right" is without any basis in fact or reason. There is no reason why a newborn baby boy should be wrapped in a blue blanket. There is no logic to the observable fact that Northern Europeans and Americans have a more highly developed sense of guilt than the Japanese. Once we sense that something powerful is constantly at work to create these attitudes and patterns of behavior, then we begin to see that many characteristics such as aggression, acquisitiveness, trust in people, or fear of spirits are deeply embedded in growing children by the people who raise them. At this point we understand how ritual, cere-monies, marriage customs, laws, social organization, and lan-guage are the means by which a culture is communicated to children and reinforced among adults.

The second stage emerges when a person begins to wonder what is true out of the enormous range of cultures and sub-cultures which are in existence—a "subculture" being a special form of a larger culture, such as the white farmer in Appalachia or the welfare recipient in the black ghetto. Since each cultural style of life makes sense to the people involved in it so that they, therefore, continue to propagate it, the tendency is to assume that what is "good, true, and beautiful" can only be defined in relation to what a particular cultural group says it is. This is the stage of radical cultural relativity—when a person believes that polygamy can be judged ethically only in relation to the society in which it is found. Many people stop here with the slogan that was widely quoted in the 1930's: "Name any form of human behavior that you think is wrong and I will show you a society where it is considered normal."

The third stage is reached when a person begins to believe that there are some things which are good and some things which are bad for human life, and to want all people to live pleasant, creative lives is a human and not a culturally bound desire. At the most fundamental level, the "good" is having enough to eat and enough social stability not to have to worry about shelter. The "good" is having an education that helps people understand the world about them and gives them confidence in their ability to shape their own affairs. The "bad" is disease, murder, war, or cultural attitudes which breed distrust. Your list may be longer or shorter, but the point is that one develops a platform from which one can judge all cultures, especially one's own. In this third stage one also thinks of ways to use the natural acculturation process to bring about the "good" for all people.

How things will go with you as you read this book only time will tell. I can only give warning that the cultural approach is heady wine and the effect may linger a long time. Let's use the authors as illustrations. John and Gwen use an informal style; some parts of this book are conversations between the two. Let me continue that style. I was present in the meeting at Greenwich, Connecticut, sponsored by the World Council of Churches, where John and Gwen met. I participated in some of the stimulating conversations that took place as we discovered we had a common interest in a cultural approach to religious education. You will note in Gwen's essays that at the time of the Greenwich meeting she was in stage two but since then has moved tentatively into stage three. At the moment she does not know exactly what facet of culture will engage her attention in the future, but she is willing to consider the possibilities of the church's being an agency of change. John, apparently, is in stage three—happily looking for ways to do two things simultaneously. One is to rethink the meaning of the Christian religion in adult terms for the contemporary situation. The other is to use what we know about the acculturation process to raise a new generation in a more adequate faith. He wants to carry on both tasks in the hurly-burly of life in a congregation. Neither John nor Gwen attempts in these essays to do more than invite you to start on the road to a discovery they have already made. They share with you their excitement and some of the pain. They do not attempt to work through the problems of this point of view for the average congregation.

All this may sound threatening, and it may cause you to try too hard to get some esoteric meaning from the book. Don't worry about these things. Just be alert to how the cultural approach works, because it is not easy. There is very little new information here, nor will you find much ideology. Rather, what John and Gwen are inviting you to do is to put on a new pair of glasses so you will see old things in new perspective. Doubtless you will have difficulties with their cultural eyeglasses, because they have not given a systematic treatment of what you see. For example, sex-role stereotyping is identified as being caused by culture—and it is. But there may also be some biochemical basis for sexual differences, which is not discussed. Is the meaning of God restricted to the acculturation process that took place in childhood? There is some evidence that one's concept of God is not so restricted; but the matter is not worked out in this book. Would it be better to raise children in a kibbutz than in a family? One could so argue on the principles discussed in this book, but the matter is not mentioned. These issues are raised not to say that the book is incomplete but simply to show that John and Gwen are more concerned that the glasses fit and that you see ... rather than with exactly what you do with your new way of perceiving life.

Groups,
Group Life,
and Religious Socialization

Section One deals with the nature of group communal life as it reflects and embodies a cultural world view. Each segment of American Christianity is a part of a deeper and wider cultural heritage from a European tradition. As such, each represents a cultural or "ethnic" community of faith.

Within economic activity cycles, in social organizational structures of family, kin, and congregation, in recurrent ceremonies and gatherings over time and space, the agreeing community of faith transmits its way of life. Socialization is used to refer to this total process. Enculturation is another term that denotes the same phenomenon. Enculturation implies the transmission of lifeways from adults to children so that they ensure that the culture continues.

The process of enculturation within our multiethnic, multiculture, multigroup American society must take place on two levels: one is exemplified in a particular congregation and religious group, the other is found on the level of nationally shared political, social, and scientific value systems. Communal life is essential for group continuation at both levels.

In this section, therefore, we explore some of the dynamics of these communal life processes and their relevance to religious socialization and education.

Chapter 1

Protestants and Roman Catholics Together

John H. Westerhoff III

A number of years ago I penned an article for the *Catechist*.[1] It raised the question: Why is it that Protestants and Roman Catholics, when it comes to educational change, keep passing each other in the night? I described what I believed to be the common educational dilemma faced by both Protestants and Roman Catholics. And then I questioned why it was that we have each tended to recommend solutions for our educational problems that the other has already demonstrated as inadequate. Finally, I put forth the challenge that we plan together for an alternative future. Numerous readers agreed, but none of us seemed to know where to begin. The editor of the *Catechist* asked me for an article that would suggest a new approach for our educational ministries. I couldn't respond because I wasn't sure what to say. But now I have a proposal, thanks to an action by the Roman Catholic hierarchy, an action stimulated by the Second Vatican Council (perhaps the most significant event in the history of the ecumenical movement).

This action was the preparation of a General Catechetical Directory. Although the Second Vatican Council adjourned in 1965, its work is not yet completed. Gradually specific measures of reform or renewal prescribed by the council are being implemented. As one response, the General Catechetical Directory has been issued.[2] Published in June 1971, the directory's aim is to promote renewal in catechesis, a pastoral activity of the church—a renewal which concerns "religious education" but is importantly understood as an integral part of the church's total renewal. My introduction to the General Catechetical Directory came through *Catechetics in Context*,[3] a commentary on the directory by Berard L. Marthaler of Catholic University. The important issues raised by this book have been more stimulating to me than almost anything else I have read on religious education in recent years.[4]

In a closing paragraph of "A Protestant Response to the General Catechetical Directory," C. Ellis Nelson remarked:

I think there are profound possibilities for a new start in religious education for all Christians if we can probe the possibilities of community for nurture. The most radical idea of all would be to conceive of a local church so working and worshipping together that they need very little formal systematic study. But that may be just the subliminal dream of a Protestant who believes that the New Testament forms some sort of norm for life in the church, as well as her theology. I would commend the idea of community, to the group planning the American Catechetical Directory, as a way to think about catechesis which may be more natural for a church than the notion of a school.[5]

With those words Nelson offers a veiled invitation to the Catholic community in America to look seriously at the concept of the church community as a possible alternative or at least a supplement to their present schooling models. I've made the same invitation to the Protestant community in *Values for Tomorrow's Children*[6] and in my essays within *A Colloquy on Christian Education*.[7] Now I'm suggesting that the General Catechetical Directory offers both Protestants and Roman Catholics a place to begin our rethinking of religious education together.

That suggestion is rooted in the historical fact that both Protestants and Catholics have, in recent history, placed most all their religious education efforts in one sort of schooling or another. And despite diverse histories, both communities today are facing somewhat identical crises—a mistrust in schooling to reach the educational ends for which they were established and a failure to have adequately educated their parishioners in the Christian faith and life. To say that a new start is called for is, I believe, to belabor the obvious. I assume there is a need to frame an alternative to our present educational programs. What

I'm recommending, therefore, is a new point of departure. That point would begin by studying the process of cultural transmission or socialization. Such a study would help us gain a new perspective on religious education or catechetics.

Such an approach is not, of course, entirely original. Some Catholic and Protestant educators are already experimenting with community models of education. Sometimes it's been called "total religious education." I have often referred to it as "holistic education" or "community-of-faith education."

My friend, Fr. Mark Heath, O.P. (whose thoughts influenced this essay), suggests that one of the most fundamental changes introduced into Catholic church life by the Vatican Council came in the form of an idea or concept. While not revolutionary, it is quite radical in the true sense of that word. The council affirmed that the local parish church is and ought to be understood as a community of love. This is a *new* emphasis. For a long time the parish church has been thought of as a service center, a place where necessary religious services (such as the sacraments and instruction) were offered to the faithful by persons who were granted the authority to offer them. It is true, of course, that many parishes, especially those with a strong ethnic identity, were in fact social communities. But, as Father Heath points out, in the ways in which Catholic life was expressed and parish functions executed, even these churches were far from actualizing true religious community.

What the Vatican Council appears to have done, without attacking the organizational structure of the church, is to reintroduce and emphasize the theological idea or concept of the people or the family of God. The result has been a new emphasis on the equality and shared responsibilities of all members of the church, lay and clerical. Speaking of the pastor, Vatican II's "Decree on the Ministry and the Life of Priests" said, "The office of the pastor is not confined to the care of the individual faithful but also properly extended to the formation of genuine Christian community." [8]

Such radical ideas establish an entirely new foundation for religious education. No longer is religious education to be primarily the authoritative declaration and teaching of those truths and laws which God has revealed for salvation. Now religious education is to focus upon the communication of faith by and through a community of believers who transmit its beliefs, attitudes, and values through the myriad ways by which they live their common life together in the world. Obviously the work of catechetics can no longer be understood as primarily the responsibility of a school. Now it must become the responsibility and work of the whole Christian community. No longer can education be primarily concerned about the teaching of beliefs and morals or even learning the contents of the scriptures. Now it is to be centered on the life and work of the community of faith.

Whether it was a conscious decision or not, I do not know. But it appears significant that the Catechetical Directory was mandated to be a decree from the pastoral office of bishops and not a declaration from the congregation for Christian education. For too long religious educators have been assigned to and accepted a limited and confining understanding of their responsibility. Catechetics was, therefore, also limited and confining. But no longer. By assigning the Catechetical Directory to those with broad pastoral concerns, everything seems to have been changed. This alone should give everyone concerned for change in religious education a reason for pause. For too long educators have tended to exclude themselves from the life of the church by permitting themselves to plan for learning primarily in the context of schooling. Thus in many churches the pastor has not been significantly involved in religious education. There were always others—religious educators—to worry about it. In Protestantism we made a like sort of error. We professionalized religious educators and granted them degrees which the clergy often felt were inferior to their own. Then the church relegated such persons to directing Sunday church schools. Usually women, they remained secondary members of the church's professional leadership, with little responsibility for the life of the faith community or its cultus. Yet because these educators existed, parish ministers typically neglected the study of religious education in seminary. When, therefore, they assumed responsibility for a parish, they often gave education a low personal priority. If they couldn't afford a trained director of religious education, a lay person would do. The clergy seemed to have concluded that religious education was someone else's responsibility. So it was that religious educators ended up directing church schools and pastors ignored religious education.

A like phenomenon seems to have occurred in the Roman Catholic Church. A religious educator is responsible for either parochial schools or some other sort of schooling (CCD) for those who do not attend parochial school. Pastors, in general, do not make religious education a primary personal aspect of their ministry. Their responsibility is to make sure catechetics is not forgotten. Most often they have responded by turning the responsibility for religious education over to others, mostly women (nuns) who have little or no responsibility or say in the general life of the parish. But all that will change if the General Catechetical Directory is taken seriously. Nuns, parish priests, and the laity will join together in rethinking religious education in the context of parish life and community. Religious education will begin to focus upon intentional religious socialization. Catechetics as the work of the whole church will find its content in the total life of the church. Pope Paul VI encouraged such an understanding when he addressed the International Catechetical Congress at Rome in September 1971:

Catechesis is a teaching that requires, more than any other teaching, the intervention of the persons concerned. It requires the living and direct work of the whole community of the church. Catechesis can be considered a testimony of faith. Now every believer is obliged to render this testimony, by professing his own faith, in deed, by example, and by words.[9]

The Catechetical Directory emphasizes an identical understanding:

The content of catechetics is found in God's word, written or handed down; it is more deeply understood and developed by the people exercising their faith under the guidance of the Magisterium, which alone teaches authentically; it is celebrated in the liturgy; it shines forth in the life of the Church, especially in the just and in the saints; and in some way it is known too from those genuine moral values which, by divine providence, are found in human society.[10]

Catechetics, therefore, includes helping people understand, deepen, and exercise their faith by participation in the community of faith, a community acting out its faith in the world. It involves participation in the liturgy; it includes observing, discovering, and enhancing the faith in the total life and work of the church; and it is concerned with uncovering the faith in the moral values of society.

The directory makes clear that catechetics—which obviously should encourage personal experience of faith and reflection on religious matters—is not complete, however, unless it results in Christian action. Christian catechesis should educate persons to assume the responsibilities of faith. And such learning, it confesses, can only take place in a community which is facing the issues of worldly Christian life by becoming involved in actual human struggles. Thus the parish life of fellowship with its tensions and disagreements, the communal facing of moral issues, personal and social, and parish action aimed at addressing such issues are the proper locus of religious education.

Continually the Catechetical Directory affirms that catechesis is not limited to a few professionals but is the task of the entire church community. But perhaps even more radical is its stand that catechesis is not just for children but in fact principally for adults, for it is through the life and action of the adult community that faith is transmitted to the next generation.

There are other important points in the directory. For example, it establishes the ritual life of the church as an essential aspect of religious education (an aspect of socialization we Protestants have almost totally ignored in our recent history). What emerges from the directory's understanding of "religious education" is an emphasis on the church as a worshiping, learning, and witnessing community of faith.

Catechesis is to be directly related to all pastoral activities: worship, parish life and fellowship, social action and service. Although it is careful not to make education into everything that happens in the life of the parish, it suggests that educators need to focus their efforts on all aspects of the church's life.[11]

In a major address to the International Catechetical Congress at Rome in September 1971, John Cardinal Wright said:

Any catechetical activity that is isolated from the ecclesial context in which it exists is destined to be inefficacious. Not parochial catechesis, catechetics in school, family instruction, conferences for special groups of believers, nor any other kind of catechetics, can be efficacious by itself. Consequently, it is unthinkable that catechetical activity be developed without connection and collaboration with other ecclesial activity. It is especially underlined that it is necessary that every catechetical activity be related to a concrete community of the faithful which lives the faith effectively.[12]

To think about or plan education from this perspective will not be an easy task for Roman Catholics or Protestants. It is unfamiliar territory for us both. Yet I see no other way for us to proceed. Education must be carried on by the total parish community, for the aim of "religious education" is for both individual growth in the faith and for the building up of the community of faith. Accomplishing this aim will be a long, slow, and perhaps painful task, but one which I recommend to all of us who desire an alternative future for the Christian community and an alternative future for religious education. It is a road we can—and, indeed, ought to—travel together. I further suggest that the place for us to begin is with Berard Marthaler's commentary on the General Catechetical Directory, *Catechetics in Context*.

Neither of us can assume that the church as it exists is the way it ought to be. Inducting persons into its life or training them only to be active members is not enough. Reform and renewal of the church is essential. Perhaps the challenge which lies before us is not primarily one of instructing children; it may well be one of converting adults. And for that end, religious education is surely not an academic enterprise. But neither is it a new task.

Berard Marthaler writes:

There is a marked difference between the catechetical activity of the early church and that of the modern church. Until the Sixth or Seventh Century catechesis was directed to adults who, having heard the gospel message, knowingly or willingly asked to join the Christian community. The time of preparation for baptism, the catechumenate, lasted several years through a period of "conversion." Later, when the practice of infant baptism became universal, the focus of catechesis began to shift to children.

The lament is not that infants and children are baptized and instructed in the faith, but that catechesis came to focus primarily if not solely on children and adolescents. Consequently, the main thrust of catechetical activity centered on the school, question-answer methods and "initiation" into the Church. The point of the Directory is that the paradigm—"the chief form"—must rather be adult catechesis. "Maturity of faith" is the goal of catechesis. Thus catechizing youngsters is not the main task but simply a prelude to the principal movement.[13]

I agree. I'd like to make conversion a major concern of religious education. Yet I know that conversion will never alone be satisfactory. As Peter Berger and Thomas Luckmann in their book, *The Social Construction of Reality*, put it:

It is only within the religious community, the *ecclesia*, that the conversion can be effectively maintained as plausible. . . . To have a conversion experience is nothing much. The real thing is to be able to keep on taking it seriously; to retain a sense of its plausibility. *This* is where the religious community comes in. It provides the indispensable plausibility structure for the new reality. In other words, Saul may have become Paul in the aloneness of religious ecstasy, but he could *remain* Paul only in the context of the Christian community that recognized him as such and confirmed the "new being" in which he now located this identity. This relationship of conversion and community is not a peculiarly Christian phenomenon. . . . One cannot remain a Muslim outside the *'umma* of Islam, a Buddhist outside the *sangha,* and probably not a Hindu anywhere outside India. Religion requires a religious community, and to live in a religious world requires affiliation with that community.[14]

The directory places an emphasis on active, conscious, genuine participation in the life of a Christian community—a Christian community of converts who live and act in the world as the faithful people of God. That's where it belongs! And that conviction implies a shift in our focus as educators to what I'd like to call "religious socialization."

Although the directory does not use that term, the educational role it attributes to the church community is in effect a description of "intentional socialization." From one point of view, all education is socialization—that is to say, a process by which an individual is initiated into a particular community, educated to its values and ideals, and led at some point—the threshold of maturity—to internalize them and adopt them for his own. And it is likewise the process by which that community sustains its understanding and way of life—that is, keeps itself faithful.

I've had a suspicion that was true for some time. The directory has reinforced and focused my suspicion. And so I now recommend that Protestants and Roman Catholics join together in considering "religious socialization" as their point of departure for planning religious education. Obviously I hope others will agree, for the most difficult part of the task remains. My hope is that the essays in this volume will help us to get started.

Chapter 2

What Is
Religious Socialization?[1]

John H. Westerhoff III

"Religious socialization" cannot be found in the contents of any theological or educational textbook with which I am familiar. As separate concepts the two terms abound; socialization has been defined in numerous ways, religion in many more. But religious socialization is yet to be defined. Now surely, definitions are not an end in themselves. Still, they do serve important purposes. Verbal clarity can give new insight and understanding. But perhaps more important than definitions are the words we choose to define. Consider the significance of main-line Protestantism's use of the words religious education, Christian education, and church education. Emphasis on each of those terms not only characterized historical periods, they shaped them.

Thus it is that I would like to highlight and seek to define religious socialization. I do so not for academic reasons but rather because of practical concern for the confused, troubled state of "education" in main-line Protestant churches (that is the COCU churches and others like them). It is my conviction that a focusing of attention on religious socialization could enable main-line Protestant Christian educators to break out of their current malaise and assist in framing an alternative future for their churches. But more of that later.

Understanding Socialization

To begin, let us consider the concept "socialization."[2] The word has been around for a long time; however, it was first given currency by social scientists in the 1930's. For some, socializa-

tion (or enculturation) is as broad as the total lifelong process
by which human culture is transmitted—culture being the shared
learned behavior (thinking, feeling, and acting) and its products
(art, law, custom, etc.) which distinguish one community of people from another. Others prefer a more narrow understanding of
the word. For them, socialization is the inculcation in children,
by their parents and the community, in the early years, of those
skills and attitudes necessary for the acquisition of particular
social roles. Little will be gained for our purpose by detailing the
multitude of definitions which lie between those two poles. What
is significant is the way in which socialization is consistently
differentiated from education.

Education is a more limited concept. While socialization includes education, education is a distinct aspect of socialization.
Education describes the explicit efforts that individuals and
groups make toward shaping the behavior of persons. Or to put it
another way, education is the "deliberate systematic and
sustained efforts to transmit or evoke knowledge, attitudes,
values, skills and sensibilities in persons." [3]

Education, then, refers to *all the intentional efforts* made by
persons and groups to aid individuals in acquiring the knowledge,
skills, and dispositions that make them more or less able and
acceptable members of a society. Schooling is a specific form
of education, a much narrower phenomenon. Socialization, on
the other hand, while including all such explicit efforts (schooling and education), also includes the formal and informal implicit
means by which a people acquire and sustain their understandings and way of life.

The anthropologist Irvin Child defines socialization as

a broad term for the whole process by which an individual born
with behavioral potentialities of an enormously wide range, is led
to develop actual behavior which is confined within a much narrower range—the range of what is customary and acceptable for him
according to the standards of his group. [4]

While most social scientists conceive of this process as lifelong
—individuals continually enter new roles and acquire new behaviors as they move through their life cycle—the crucial and

perhaps irreversible influences of early experience are emphasized.

Underlying most all understandings of socialization are three fundamental assumptions:

First: All perceptions and behaviors are learned in a social context, through interaction of persons with family, kin, peers, and significant others, and through participation in a community or ethnic group—that is, a group bearing a more or less distinctive culture.

Second: The existence and vitality, over time, of a society or a group within a society depends upon consensus among its members as to an understanding of life and appropriate ways of thinking, feeling, and acting.

Third: Every people transmit their way of life, from one generation to another, through formal and informal, conscious and unconscious, spontaneous and planned means.

Consistent with these assumptions, let me suggest a definition: Socialization is the lifelong formal and informal ways one generation seeks to sustain and transmit its understanding and way of life; seeks to induct its young into and reinforce for its adults a particular set of values and responsible adult roles; and seeks to help persons develop self-identity through participation in the life of a people with their more or less distinctive ways of thinking, feeling, and acting.

Understanding Religion

My definition of socialization surely doesn't intend to be definitive, but I hope it provides us with enough understanding of half our concept, "religious socialization," that we can turn to the more difficult word, religion.[5] While socialization is not a common word in everyone's daily vocabulary, religion is. That complicates the task of definition. Religion brings to mind various images for different people. For some it means belief in God or bowing one's head for prayer. For others, it means an argument over doctrine. For still others, it means magic and superstition. To make our problem more complex, there is little agreement among those who strive to use the word with more precision. In *The Meaning and End of Religion,* Wilfred Cantwell Smith traces how, in the West, religion has meant successively and simultaneously at least four different things: (1) that personal piety or pervasive disposition that permeates and gives coherence to a person's strivings and responses, (2) the *ideal* system of beliefs, practices, and values that constitute a particular people's tradition of piety, (3) the *actual* or *empirical* embodiment of that ideal system in the lives and practices of historical individuals and communities, and (4) a generic category epitomized in a universal dimension of human life and self-consciousness—"religion in general." [6]

Each of these usages alone poses difficulties for me. The last, for example, I find too broad and abstract to be helpful. The first, on the other hand, comes closer to what I would characterize as faith, or that basic all-encompassing frame of mind (world view and value system) which colors a person's whole way of behaving. Faith, as I use the word, is the expression of meaning revealed in a person's life-style, or that foundation upon which persons live their lives, that point of centeredness or ultimacy that underlies and is expressed abstractly in a world view and value system or, more concretely, in the ways persons think, feel, and act.

My understanding of *religion* refers to those concrete communal expressions of faith which are embodied in the life of a people—a community of faith. Religion is faith given shape, form, and content. As such, religion refers to the myths, symbols, rituals, actions, and activities of that community which is the bearer of a particular understanding and way of life. Thus religion seems best understood as a combination of the second and third possibilities proposed by Smith—that is, as the communal expression of faith in institutional forms or the embodiment of a world view and value system in the lives and practices of historical individuals and communities.

Humans are incorrigibly religious. That is, they require an understanding of life, an awareness of their place in it, and behavioral guides by which they intend to live. Religion demonstrates the needs of persons to have an understanding of life and their lives and to express that understanding in personal and corporate ways. Religion, with its communities, rituals, myths, symbols, expressions of belief, organizational patterns, activities, and behaviors, answers this need by communicating, reinforcing, and providing a context for the development and sustenance of personal faith. In turn, the faith of a people is expressed and mediated through and within the context of historical social forms of community life and tradition which I call religion. Religion is faith made real or faith actualized through concrete historical expressions which have meaning for a people and are an integral part of their culture.

Religious Socialization Defined

What then is religious socialization? Let me hazard a definition: *Religious socialization is a process consisting of lifelong formal and informal mechanisms, through which persons sustain and transmit their faith (world view, value system) and life-style.* This is accomplished through participation in the life of a tradition-bearing community with its rites, rituals, myths, symbols, expressions of beliefs, attitudes and values, organizational patterns, and activities.

Religious education, on the other hand, can be defined as: those deliberate systematic and sustained efforts of a community of faith which intentionally aim at enabling persons and groups to evolve particular ways of thinking, feeling, and acting.

The fundamental difference between religious socialization and religious education should be obvious. The latter is intentional, while the former includes both the intentional and the unintentional. Socialization is more inclusive. There is another difference, not so much inherent in definition as in the perceptions of church educators. For most, socialization is at best a blurred image; education is clearer but tends to refer almost exclusively to church schooling and its printed curricula, youth fellowships and their stated programs, confirmation and pastor's classes, and perhaps particular programs labeled adult education. Now all these are surely "deliberate systematic and sustained efforts." They are education.

But my contention is that many educators, in their concern for schooling, printed resources, classes, and programs, have tended to be unaware of the "hidden curriculum" which always unconsciously underlies all their intentional efforts. For example, in research on church school curriculum and anti-Semitism, Bernhard Olson in his massive study *Faith and Prejudice* (1963) documents that when church bodies set out deliberately to teach about other groups, the results are reasonably satisfactory. It is in the implicit anti-Semitism, when teaching about the crucifixion of Jesus or the Pharisees, that prejudicial teaching occurs. Similarly, studies in sex-role stereotyping have revealed blatant sexism in church school curricula. The case seems, however, to be the same. When curriculum writers intentionally set out to deal with this issue in church school resources they did pretty well at encouraging the healthy growth and development of men and women and thereby avoided negative sex-role stereotyping. However, almost every other aspect of these resources supported and reinforced the very negatives they strived to overcome in particular lessons.[7]

Another serious problem results from the concentration by some church educators on religious education as schooling. Unconsciously this concentration tends to remove from their purview social interaction and social organization—the rites, rituals, symbols, myths, organizational patterns, activities, and other social and cultural aspects of the church's life. The price paid is high. During the past twenty-five years few of these important aspects of socialization have been used by educators as contexts for learning around which intentional (educational) efforts needed to be planned and actualized.

The results of this neglect are well known. A tremendous gap has evolved between what we teach and what we are, what we preach and what we live. I suggest that we have often failed in our educational efforts because we neglected the nature of socialization—not because we were poor educators. Therefore, I recommend that we initially turn our attention from "religious education" to "religious socialization." Not because I believe that education is unimportant, but because I believe we need to bring the hidden dimensions of socialization into view and include them in our educational activity. With a new consciousness of how persons acquire their understanding and way of life, we can turn freshly to plan for education—that is, make the whole life of the church part of our "deliberate systematic and sustained efforts." I've named this wholistic educational process "intentional religious socialization."

Exploring Religious Socialization in the Church

To repeat my all-inclusive and broad definition: Religious socialization is a process consisting of lifelong formal and informal mechanisms, through which persons sustain and transmit their faith (world view, value system) and life-style, and this, recall, is accomplished through participation in the life of a tradition-bearing community with its rites, rituals, myths, symbols, expressions of belief, attitudes and values, organizational patterns, and activities. In order to make clearer the content of this definition, let me try to describe a few aspects of religious socialization by suggesting some questions to be asked about the church.

To begin, we can explore the ways in which an environment socializes. For example, the interior and exterior structures of church buildings, their location and use in and by the neighborhood community, are contexts for socialization. The most important thing to do is not overlook the obvious; that is, take nothing for granted.

Here is an exercise in observation: For a short time try to drop all your preconceived ideas about what churches and neighborhoods "ought to" look like. Now attempt to observe the church building without set value judgments. Just note and describe. Is the church new or old? How well is it maintained? Is there special significance to how it was built? Are there religious symbols on the building? What do they mean to people? How is the building used? When is it used? Who uses it? What is its relationship to the surrounding environment?

People are socialized by the space and ecology in which they live. For example, we come to understand that the church exists to serve particular persons in particular ways by the relationship of the church (as a physical presence) to the persons and other physical objects in its environment. It is difficult for participants to learn that the church exists for the liberation of the poor and oppressed if the church building exists in an urban environment of poor oppressed peoples but in no significantly liberating way makes contact with their lives. But you can't always be sure of the effect of an environment. For this reason it is important to ask local people how they understand the church's presence in their neighborhood. In this way you can check out your hypotheses on what is being learned from the experiences of persons with and within the church.

Moving to the interior environment of the church, the same sorts of questions can be asked. What is the significance of the room arrangement, the religious symbols and artifacts? Has the interior space of the church or its rooms ever been changed? How and why? For what purposes, by whom, when, and under what circumstances is different space occupied? Do the rooms have names? What is the main function and use of each?

It might be interesting to note that often rooms in the church are named after wealthy men in the church who contributed money for the building—that is, with the exception of the ladies' parlor, used only for tea, and the kitchen, which were given by the women's fellowship. What does this naming teach about the values of Christian community and the New Testament's professed bias on behalf of the poor and oppressed?

What we need to remember is that the architecture of socialization has more to do with the church in its environment than with the building of church schools. The church building itself, set in the community, is a "schoolhouse." It reveals its people to themselves, tells them about their beliefs, attitudes, and values. Christian education has been thought of as taking place mainly within the confines of a classroom. Church school buildings have been regarded as the citadels of religious knowledge and the nurseries of faith. However, the most extensive socializing force imaginable is the overall environment in which people live. The church is a classroom without walls, offering for people of all ages—especially the impressionable young—a boundless hidden curriculum. We need to discover the interior and exterior environments of the church as socializing—learning—resources.

To explore further an understanding of religious socialization, we can consider the primary group relationships, role models, and status figures found in every congregation. In all associations there are divisions of labor. People assume different roles; status is assigned. Different contributions are expected of children, adolescents, adults, and old people. Those roles assigned by the community, as well as the adult models offered to children by those who accept particular roles, are important for religious socialization.

For example, at present we are witnessing a conflict in role definition in the church as well as society. A movement for the liberation of women is attempting to alter the parameters within which women's roles have been defined. This is a theological and ethical concern. The community of faith cannot avoid such issues. The roles played by women in the church are important.

Roles are the grooves in which behavior is channeled. They are essential aspects of socialization. For example, some persons are assigned the role of leader, others follower. Some are assigned responsibility and power, others are given particular jobs to do or decisions to implement. We need to explore the roles persons play in the life of the church. Who plays what roles? Who is excluded? Who determines what roles will be played? What new roles are persons seeking? Who is holding them back or encouraging them? What roles are persons as Christians encouraged to play "in the world"? What roles do they actually play? If there is a difference, why?

The attempt to further clarify and describe religious socialization could go on. If it did I would include a discussion of such things as the activities and programs of the church, the life-styles of its people, the use of time and money by the church and its members, and the myths, symbols, rites, and rituals of the church.

Family and Peer Groups

The aspects of religious socialization so far described and the questions suggested for exploration are not meant to be comprehensive. They are only intended to help clarify our definition. However, before I close, I'd like to make a few other comments. Obviously a person's most significant experiences are those in her or his family, particularly in the earliest years. The first and most important socializing agency is the family. The manner in which persons relate to one another and the manner in which parents relate to their children are central to religious socialization. More important than formal indoctrination are the subtle attitudes and frames of reference that are acquired by children as a result of the way they are treated. The family is the first unit with which the child has continuous contact. It is a primary group whose close, intense, and enduring emotional attachments are basic to all experience and perceptions. A person's faith, world view, beliefs, attitudes and values cannot be understood without reference to the family and to the early years of child-rearing.

Parents through their decisions on where to live, whom to have for friends, and even which programs to watch on TV influence the child's religious growth and development. Within the family a child learns values, sentiments, statuses and role expectations. A child's first rewards and punishments, first images of personhood, and first models of behavior are experienced in family settings. Needless to say, socialization cannot be understood without a careful analysis of the family and family life.

Of almost equal significance for socialization, particularly in American culture, is the peer group. Unlike the institutions of the school, church, and community, which tend to represent the established order and conventional values, the peer group often socializes persons into new emerging values, new understandings of life, and new actions. The peer group serves to expand the social horizons of children and make them into more complex persons. Through such groups young people become independent of parents and other adult authorities. In the peer group, they develop new attitudes and identify new role models. The peer group has its own pattern of thoughts and behavior for transmitting an understanding of life and a person's place in it. Increasingly significant are the processes of socialization which take place within these associations. Neither it, the family, nor the school and community can be ignored in understanding socialization.

However, while my definition of religious socialization does not intend to neglect these important socializing forces for religion, it does focus on that socialization which occurs within communities of faith. I have done this consciously because I firmly believe that, without a community of faith to support, sustain, and transmit the family's faith and values, religious socialization faces an almost impossible task. As Berger and Luckmann put it, "Religion requires a religious community, and to live in a religious world requires affiliation with that community." [8] So, while socialization in the family and peer group is important for religious faith and life, an intentional community of faith remains the essential key to religious socialization. The emphasis of my definition is therefore on such community.

Faith is fostered and given meaning by the way those who claim that faith live and act in community. Persons develop their religious self-identity by participation in the actions of a community of faith. That process goes on throughout life but is particularly important in the early years, when a child observes and identifies with acceptable role models, and later in adolescence, when young people are encouraged to participate with adults in performing actions sanctioned by the community as expressions of faith. Surely we must experience and act out our faith before we can fully comprehend it. This is done in community and through institutional expressions. The acquisition of faith requires opportunities for appropriate action and experience. These can best be actualized in a family of families, a community of faith, with its rites, rituals, symbols, myths, beliefs, attitudes, and values.

Our definition of religious socialization therefore remains: Religious socialization is a process consisting of lifelong formal and informal mechanisms, through which persons sustain and transmit their faith (world view, value system) and life-style, and thus is accomplished through participation in the life of a tradition-bearing community with its rites, rituals, myths, symbols, expressions of belief, attitudes and values, organizational patterns, and activities.

The Limitations of Religious Socialization

Before I close this essay, I want to acknowledge the implicit danger in our discussion of religious socialization (and my briefer comments on religious education). Concentrating on concepts such as socialization or education can imply a deterministic understanding of persons and their acquisition of faith. That possibility needs to be addressed. Joseph Fichter in his presidential address to the Society for the Scientific Study of Religion wisely questions this basic methodological assumption, an assumption which has tended to inform the social sciences—namely, that man's behavior is determined.[9]

It is almost too easy, or perhaps a natural consequence of writing about religious socialization, to assume that we know exactly how faith and values are acquired. As Peter Berger remarked, "Socialization is now seen not just as the process by which the self becomes integrated into society but rather as the process in which the self is actually produced."[10] The experimental fact is that persons always seem to present us with the "person-factor," an unknown which interacts in the socialization process, calling any deterministic assumptions into question. The experiential fact is that as persons we know that we are not merely the result of outside forces which make us into their choosing. We are free and responsible. We respond and react. We discern and decide. We initiate action. In short, we are more than mere players of preexistent or determined roles; we are meaning makers and value choosers. It seems as if even the most deterministic forms of attempted socialization cannot predetermine a person's faith, world view, or values.[11]

The classic observation of Ruth Benedict—that we are both the creator (the producer) and the creature (the product) of our culture—cannot be repeated too often. Thus Joseph Fichter comments, "It is difficult to understand why there has been a continuing focus on man as creature and product of culture and a continuing neglect of man as creator and producer of culture."[12] That neglect we do not intend to perpetuate. Even as I affirm the truth of religious socialization, I want also to affirm that the human being is at the same time an active-interactive person who not only acquires but produces faith.

What, therefore, I have been discussing in this striving to understand religious socialization is part of a process, that part for which we as educators can (and in fact morally must) take responsibility. But only that and no more. So we return to the beginning. I began by affirming the need to direct our attention first to religious socialization and then to a widened concern for a more wholistic approach to religious education or, as I've named it, "intentional religious socialization." I suggested that this would enable us to break out of our current malaise in religious education and assist us in framing an alternative future for the church. What this contention implies is that we are not helpless. There is something we can do. But we enter that responsibility fully aware of the limitations of our endeavors, trusting in persons and in God for the wise actualization of our sometimes feeble efforts. Mindful we can be. Little else can be required of us.

Gwen Comments

John's prerequisite that religious socialization takes place within a community of faith closely approximates the dictum in anthropology that culture learning takes place within a cultural community. In fact, the anthropologist will tell you that the human community is the *basic cell* of culture and of human social organization. All humans are biosocial creatures, and to be human they must be community dwellers—as bees to be bees must live in social groups and cooperate as hives to fulfill the biogram of their species.

Humans have a biogram as well, shared with all living creatures, of birth, growth, reproduction, and death. But in addition we have also a "culture-gram" to live out, composed of all the symbolic meanings and sacred interpretations that each tradition places on the simple biological events.

The culture-gram is a set of patterned meanings, expectations, and behaviors that the individual infant receives as a member of a social group. In teaching my introductory class in cultural anthropology, I compare this package to the brown envelope one receives at the beginning of a convention or conference. Inside are all the rules, schedules, and extra information one needs to be a participant in that conference. After careful reading and absorption, one has all the necessary formal rules to function in the group. During the convention itself, however, one is often influenced by chance meetings with friends, new data being given out, accidental occurrences, and just individual preference and variability in the way the conference unfolds.

Growing up in a cultural-community matrix, interacting with parents, siblings, relatives, teachers, and friends, the child is given his or her instructions, the formal rules (and the ways to break the rules) that are needed to become an adult in that society.

John has elaborated on the theme that all the aspects of space, time, and social arrangements communicate to the child just how to be an adult in each particular subcultural community—or within each denomination, or within each "community of faith." My following article on kin and congregation attempts to give one example of the dynamics of this transmission process as culture persists tenaciously down, down through the generations.

Chapter 3

The Sacred Community—
Kin and Congregation
in the Transmission of Culture [1]

Gwen Kennedy Neville

Where is the community of faith in American urban life? We read
of the mobile population, of the isolated nuclear family, of the
breakdown of the ethnic church as a community center. Is there a
viable social support group, we ask, that remains connected to
cultural ties and, specifically, to the religious group? These
questions were the ones that propelled me into my research
project on the Southern Presbyterians, a search for answers that
has now lasted for three years and has included two separately
funded studies of cultural persistence and cultural transmission.

In the earliest phase of work, I was primarily interested in the
dynamics of cultural transmission and the preservation of religious groups as entities with "a sense of peoplehood." The
obvious persistence of cultural groups as internal pockets
throughout the nation seemed to contradict the news from sociologists that the community was breaking down and the church
was dying. Even as I read of the secular gospel, the death of
God, and the privatization of religion, I kept being faced with
ethnic enclaves, with strong and viable church groups, and with
individuals whose early fundamentalist training kept them well
within the Protestant fold as the new morality came and went,
passing them by.

Fortunately for me, as a cultural anthropologist, I was observing
the secularization and urbanization process from within one fascinating culture. The region of my concern prides itself with the
final resistance to a national or civil religion. Within this area a
mosaic of sparkling European cultures persist as small sects

in rural towns and as powerful regional denominations encompassing several states. The region is, of course, the American South. Its cultural diversity is enough to dazzle an anthropologist from Mars, and yet, amazingly, most of these internal cultural patches and pockets of Europe and Africa remain untouched and unobserved by the clinical eye of the outside anthropologist or ethnographer.

This is in part due to the avidity with which the members of the anthropological club (a religion in itself) have been busy taking captive on paper all the world's primitive peoples, including a sizable portion of the American Indian tribes. As a result of their preoccupation with "primitives," anthropologists have only recently begun to describe the Euro-American subgroups all around us.

The ethnographer's task is to describe and elucidate and then to leave alone. In describing and elucidating the social organization and sacred meanings of my own tribe in American Christianity, I have sought to be sympathetic and gentle, to participate in the culture as observer, to analyze with a measure of compassion, and then to leave the good people alone to carry on the unfolding process of their communal life.

I have sought neither to judge nor to condone. I have simply provided a mirror—or painted a picture, perhaps. As any artist or photographer, I have caught those parts that interested me. And as any scientist, I have subjected my observational data to the most careful scrutiny in an attempt to fit together pieces that help shed meaning on larger questions in the search for explanations of more all-pervading systems of social and cultural reality.

The Persistence of Cultural Subgroups in American Denominations

To begin, let me say that my starting point as a student of culture is to discuss and describe the Christian denominational groups in America as each one representing a continuing European cultural tradition.[2] We assume a strong influence of Mediterranean culture within Roman Catholicism, even in Irish Catholicism, which is preserving some basic Mediterranean values and structures superimposed on a Celtic cultural base. The Reformed tradition, on the other hand, is seen as growing out of a northern

European cultural pattern of homogeneous peasant villages—where all people were already equal and shared in the communal life of planting and harvest and village government for thousands of years before Roman Christianity was introduced. There are also separate cultural strains within Reformation Christianity—the Anabaptists of German origin, who have diversified into various sects in the United States; the Congregationalists, equal villagers from East Anglia, whose ancestors were of Northern European Saxon village stock; the English feudal landowners, framing their own form of Catholic-English Christianity that fit so nicely with the hierarchy of the feudal and Southern plantation universe; and, among numerous others, the stern and sabbatarian Scottish Presbyterians, whose Celtic clan system and centrality of family is fused into a covenant between God and the federated families resulting in the new People of God.

All these groups are present within the generalized culture of "White Anglo-Saxon Protestants"—a misnomer, of course, because some of these are not of Anglo or Saxon ancestry at all but spring from a multitude of European cultural stocks. At any rate, subgroups exist and, in my view, are partially composed of European cultural configurations. Each one can be studied from this model, and each of their formal, stylized ritual behaviors will be seen to mirror separate themes and world views. For instance, the order of worship in an Anglican-Episcopal service is ordered and formal in its prescribed prayerbook liturgy. Each participant knows the exact script for each Sunday of the church calendar. The priest is the head and the initiator of activity; the congregation responds. This sequence of actions within the worship service is an accurate reflection of the feudal universe, of the master-servant relationship, and of orderly and efficient channels of upward communication. Meanwhile, the worship service of a Quaker meeting assumes equal access to the deity, and the corresponding interaction pattern is relatively spontaneous, with any number of participants initiating prayers or requests as they feel so moved.

In the face of great assimilation pressures and the recurrent waves of so-called "secularization," it seems astounding that denominations have persisted as cultural entities. Their existence and viability is a testimony to the tenacity and fierce persistence of culture over time—carried in the heads of the culture-bearers across the Atlantic and including a total inventory of ritual and social forms that could be reestablished in the communities now transplanted.

In order for each of these European denominational subcultures to exist and to continue older forms of religion brought along with older European culture forms, certain prerequisites were necessary. One of these is that the group members actually identify themselves as members of that people. A member of the Amish sect will look, think, feel, and act Amish; and an observer gets signals of Amishness from the person's clothing, appearance, and life-style. It is less easy to distinguish Presbyterians from Methodists, but, in fact, in the lives of many individuals their denominational identity is very close to their sense of selfhood. Some New England Congregationalists present a total life-style and sense of self that presumes individual autonomy and personal determination within a congregational context. Southern Methodists quickly defend a world view based on the ethic of work and of individual personal salvation. The holiness sects in the South that use snake handling as an aid in getting the spirit have formed a tight core of relationships and an identity that is separate from surrounding holiness sects. Every cultural group ever studied, in fact, has one word for humans which refers to *ourselves* and a different word referring to *the others.* Milton Gordon calls this in-group feeling "a sense of peoplehood."[3] This concept is useful in understanding the often misunderstood word *ethnos,* from which we get ethnic and ethnicity. *Ethnos* refers to cultural heritage, shared traditions, a way of life. Used in this sense, all religious denominations are in a sense ethnic and all participants are ethnics.

A second requirement for group life to persist is that there be ways of providing and maintaining this ethnicity by shared institutions and social networks and by shared ceremonies and rituals. We most often think of an ethnic group as those hyphenated Americans who have local neighborhood ghettos, local parishes, and local delicatessens along with ethnic insurance companies, political lobbies, and protective organizations to encapsulate them from birth to death. This is one way of maintaining and transmitting culture and encapsulating individuals and families. There are other equally powerful social institutions to encapsulate white Protestants. These include all-white culturally distinct churches, residential suburbs, city businessmen's organizations, country clubs, debutante societies, private schools, and often the divided worlds of local troops of scouts or local branches of libraries and YMCAs.

Denominations provide particularly useful cultural encapsulators. Even though they operate formally only on Sunday and intermittently during the week, the social networks forged by co-participation in rituals and sacred ceremonies are strong, and in many cities it is plausible that a newcomer find a physician, dentist, service station, cleaner, grocer, and potential business customers within the web of congregational and denominational life. I am not satisfied with the current data on the operation of this network, and I hope to see further research in the near future on its exact mechanisms.

A third prerequisite for cultural continuity is for the social group to reproduce itself in the next generation by (1) finding suitable marriage partners for the young people and (2) providing ways to enculturate the offspring of these unions. Both social reproduction through mating properly and cultural reproduction by the process of socializing the young are necessary to produce a viable ongoing community. In such a community children will grow up to be like other adults of this *ethnos;* they will have absorbed from all the informal and formal educational signals the set of rules for being a full participant in the culture.

If a group possesses these features, a person belonging to such a group is encapsulated from birth to death in a protective covering of relationships based on his or her group membership. Previous studies have assumed that this encapsulation must encompass all types and ranges of activities in order to classify the group as "ethnic." This assumption quickly spotlights the slum, the Indian reservation or urban enclave, the Jewish or black ghetto, or the suburban gilded ghetto as loci within which totally separate cultural worlds obviously exist. Among white Protestant middle-class Americans we find the impression of assimilation or nonethnic associational and occupational patterns. However, if one closely looks at the personal, kinship, and religious areas of these seemingly assimilated individuals, new data emerge on encapsulation. Individuals who work together side by side in factories and in bureaucracies may during leisure hours live in totally separate cultural worlds from one another in terms of meanings and values as well as in interactions with ceremonial communities of other Methodists, Baptists, and Presbyterians. A form of encapsulation does in fact exist in these white Anglo-Saxon groups, but it is a symbolic and ritual encapsulation that is expressed around significant individual and group transitions and events. Work on the significance of these events for the individual and the group by Turner [4] following the pioneer theories of Van Gennep [5] suggests that within the rites of passage and other rituals are found an intensely powerful mode for enculturation of the individual and the continuity of his or her cultural loyalties.

The social structural separateness and the cultural separateness both reinforced by gatherings and rituals over a transgenerational time period lead now to an examination of this type of group as a form of human community. This form of cultural interaction will be called the "ethnic community." Among white Protestant Americans each group, or web of subgroups, will have separate culturally defined patterns of behavior. The residence pattern for all of these, however, appears to be that of the scattered nuclear family household with only two generations present. On Sunday or other weekly church gathering days a wider network of families emerges at the congregational level, with a three-generational depth but not necessarily kin-based. At yearly kin-based gatherings which often are connected with religious holidays and events, an even wider net appears.

If viewed in this model, as a form of community, the ethnic group then might be identified and better understood by focusing on its significant gathered ceremonials as a locus within which cultural traditions and classic community-cultural forms will reappear. These ceremonial gatherings will be the only place where a significant cultural group assemblage appears in our now highly mobile society. It is within these ceremonial gatherings that an otherwise invisible religion is expressed visibly through symbolic behavior.

Ceremonials centering around the life crises are one point of ritual regathering—when a new baby is born, absent kin appear to pay homage or attend a baptism; at weddings, all kin within reasonable range congregate at the core of the ceremonial; and a funeral draws the largest attendance of all. Another point of ritual assemblage might be centered on group values and group

groups of siblings and often have been in one family for the seventy years of the community's existence, over two to three generations. The conference center buildings, too, reflect a historical and cultural emphasis. The earlier ones are all built of native stone by local mountain craftsmen, many of whom are of Scottish ancestry themselves. An old Scottish craft known as "dry-stone dyking," of building stone walls with no mortar, is evident in walls and fireplaces throughout the cove.

While only a few thousand of the 945,000 members of the regional Southern Presbyterian denomination attend Montreat every year, its influence is felt in every congregation as a mode of coordinating activities and reestablishing ties among an otherwise widely scattered interurban network of people.

Among the Montreat goers are two distinct groups: the "cottage people" and the "conference people." Those whom I call "core Presbyterians" are the families who own a cottage. There are 418 cottages in all. The cottage owners are largely upper-middle-class professional families, owners of businesses and mills, and Presbyterian ministers. They are proud of their ancestry of devout churchmen, all Scotch-Irish and Scottish Presbyterian. The women of the cottage families come in June with the children and spend the entire summer, with visits from the husband on weekends and during his vacation. Daughters come to spend long periods of time with their mothers, bringing along their own children to play and get acquainted with cousins.

Among the cottage families deep ties exist that have grown out of many successive summers of play and visiting. A supervised program for children, known as "the clubs," provides structured activities and games for ages five to fifteen, with college students from the long-term Montreat families serving as paid club leaders. These young adults are hand-picked from a large number of applicants to ensure that they are the best possible counselors and teachers for the task of passing on the culture to the young. Within the club groups fast friendships are formed that last throughout life. These friendships are reported to be the closest friends the participants ever have. This can be explained by Turner's work on *communitas*,[8] in which he examines the sacredness of associations and lasting friendships formed during transitional periods in the ritual process. This will not be news to those who still hold dear their college roommates, their fraternity brothers and sorority sisters, or the members of a teen-age clique of long ago.

A second circle of participants at Montreat surrounds the inner core of cottage people. These are the conference attendants, active church persons who are not descendants of older families and those whose cultural identity may be less centrally fixed to the Presbyterian way of life. These participants stay in hotels designed for a transient conference population and rarely mix with the core families of cottage people.

The cottage people were of particular interest to me as I sought tools for defining and delineating the dynamics of the scattered ethnic community. It is this central core of 418 extended families—an estimated 4,000 to 5,000 individuals in all—who are at the center of Presbyterian denominational life throughout the South. It is this inner circle of interrelated families who claim descent from Scotland and the early Covenanters, who control access to the important Southern "First Church" pulpits, who teach at the seminaries and church colleges, who serve as elders, ministers, and as denominational-level church board executives, and who have provided the social network of marriage ties that preserve the structural isolation of the Southern Presbyterians from other Protestant groups.

The core community of Presbyterians qualifies for definition as "ethnic" through the shared emphasis on a common racial and national origin and an intense feeling of "peoplehood." In addition, their common participation together in weekly worship services and congregational activities and their annual shared community life at Montreat over a transgenerational period serve to encapsulate them in a kinship-based ceremonial cocoon which goes from birth to death. The two central cultural themes uniting this group into a community with a sense of peoplehood are the twin emphases on the family and the church. Kinship and the tradition of the Covenant have been fused into a world view which perceives the universe as orderly and well planned, with human-kind as a great extended family under the fatherhood of God. Kinship and the Covenant are treated here as ideology and also as behavior. The dynamics of the preservation of community form and of patterns of grouping over time are made clearer by looking closely at these meanings and accompanying behaviors within the Presbyterian world view.

Kinfolk and Ancestors

The first strong unifying theme in the shared world view of the Montreat cottage people is their emphasis on descent from a group of ancestors who entered this continent from Scotland and the north of Ireland in the eighteenth and early nineteenth centuries. These immigrants were essentially Scottish Presbyterians of the dissenting, or "Covenanting," tradition in the southwest of Scotland and throughout the Lowlands. Many had first emigrated to Ulster Plantation between 1610 and 1710 before leaving for the American colonies. In this country they were branded Scotch-Irish because of this one-hundred-year stopover, but there is no evidence to suggest widespread intermarriage with the Celtic Irish, who were Catholic and remained bitter enemies of the transplanted Lowland Scots.[9]

The migration stream of early settlers leads from Philadelphia and the Susquehanna Valley downward into the Shenandoah Valley and outward onto the Carolina Piedmont. By 1790 the Carolina upcountry was heavily populated with Scots Presbyterians—about 100,000, according to Leyburn.[10]

The Presbyterians had moved as family clusters and as whole congregations, bringing along their minister—or in many cases coming with him as the organizer. Each congregation, then, consisted of a minister of the Church of Scotland and his small flock of three to four extended family groups of small farmers and, in some cases, merchants and townsmen. The settlement pattern was predominantly that of scattered farms with the church building at the center of a rural neighborhood. Here at the worship service on Sunday morning the mainstay of interfamily communication took place.

Because of the small size of local congregations and their kin-based nature, there were not enough marriage partners to go around at the time young people were ready to be matched. It was during times of joint meetings between congregations that matches were made, especially at the large joint services held in fall and spring for preaching, communion, and "dinner on the grounds."

In the contemporary rural Piedmont, two types of joint meetings continue to be held. One is a meeting of two or more congregations for preaching services and joint communion. The second, for all the children of one congregation, is known variously as church homecoming, the May Meeting, or the October Meeting. These are seasonal gatherings at which time all the kinfolk return to their home church (congregation of birth) to visit the family for several days and renew extended kin ties.

A strong emphasis on descent from hallowed ancestors is evidenced in these meetings. All people who have ancestors buried in the graveyard are expected to return for the occasion, and one of the preliminary activities on a Saturday before the meeting Sunday is to clean the graveyard and put fresh flowers on the ancestors' graves. In northern Appalachia this custom is still followed, under the label of Graveyard Reunion, and has recently been studied by Simpkins as an example of Scottish cultural persistency in America.[11]

In the Piedmont South this custom of joint meetings between Presbyterian congregations became the integrating key to the retention of a tight kin network over time. Other family gathering patterns lend themselves to endogamous marriage. These include the customs of "visiting," of life-crisis ceremonies, and of the family reunion.

"Visiting" is the practice of a young mother in returning to her girlhood home in summer with her children to visit her own mother for several weeks or longer. During this period, mother-daughter ties are reinforced and strengthened, sisters retain contact and strengthen ties to each other, and the young cousins grow up playing together each summer at Grandmother's house. Cousins in earlier days married each other. More recently, the children marry those to whom they have been introduced over long periods—children of the mother's girlhood friends who are visiting their own grandmother.

A second form of family gathering is held for celebration of the life-crisis events: baptism, marriage, and funerals. At these occasions kin and family solidarity are reinforced by cooperation in planning and carrying out the religious service, by the custom of staying over for several days to visit, and by bringing food and gifts, which of course has to be reciprocated later when the giver is involved in a similar transition. Many informants report courting individuals whom they met while being wedding attendants for a kinsman or friend.

A special annual gathering of the greater family provides the epitome of family ceremonial life. This gathering, still held today among some Southern Presbyterian families, is known as the family picnic or family reunion. The custom is also shared by Southern Methodists and Baptists in rural areas, but the Presbyterians seem to emphasize to a far greater degree the descent aspect from one common ancestor, rather than just the laterality of kinship relations. Large family picnics are attended by from 100 to 400 individuals. The meeting is often held outdoors at a church or church camp or at Montreat. After the visiting and eating, a master of ceremonies introduces the "head" of each family segment. The head of each family, the oldest person in the nearest generation to the ancestor, then introduces his or her children and grandchildren. Wives and husbands are mentioned in passing, but they are definitely not included in the descent chain.

It is the ancestor focus which has led me to classify the family form of this cultural group with the anthropological label "cognatic descent group." [12] All relatedness is traced through descent from one common ancestor, who stands at the apex of a great cone under which his children are each one head of subsidiary cones. It appears to be closely related to the Scottish system of *clann*, which is itself a Gaelic word meaning "children of." All the "children of" an individual by blood descent (both male and female equally) are members of the cognatic lineage or *clann*. While they carry the surname of the father's *clann*, each child is also a member of the mother's descent group and often carries that surname as a first or given name and is addressed by that name as a way of keeping mother's lineage as visible and significant.

The world of kinfolk and of Presbyterian ties places a premium on the role of the mother in handing down the traditions and bringing up children. A beautiful structural complementarity exists in which both male and female activities are necessary for the culture to survive and be passed on. Males hold respected public world positions in the church, the mills, industries, and businesses dominating the business and religious interests of the South. The females are meanwhile taught to devote themselves to the arts of the home, of child-rearing, and the improvement of school and community welfare. The males inhabit the outside world, the females the protected inner world of family and kin.

The role of the mother is crucial in teaching and caring for the young, introducing them to the proper marriage mates by bringing them each summer to Montreat, and arranging and supervising the wedding. She appears again at the homecoming of the newborn infant, sits on the porch at her daughter's Montreat house in her waning years, and at her death designates for her daughters all her own sacred home objects of silver, table china, and personal jewelry. At the death of the aged mother the sorrow is great, and her gravestone carries glowing epitaphs of having been a "virtuous woman, whose children shall rise up and call her blessed."

The importance of ancestors and of family ties over time are spotlighted in the second dominant idea of Presbyterianism— that of the Covenant People. In order to fully appreciate the contemporary communal life, it is necessary to get a historical perspective from early Scottish days.

Covenant and Covenant People

The original Presbyterians were children of the Scottish Reformation, the sixteenth- and seventeenth-century struggles in Scotland to establish the Reformed church over against the Episcopacy. In the southwest farming regions of Scotland the resistance took the form of meeting secretly in the forest to sign *banns,* or treaties, in which participants promised to fight together until they established their True Religion. These signers and their followers became known as Covenanters and their cause as Covenanting. The Covenant idea is based on the Old Testament notion that an all-powerful God has offered to save his chosen people from the wicked world. Their agreement to serve God in return for his mercy and grace is known as the Covenant. The Covenant of Works often refers to the Old Testament, and the Covenant of Grace refers to the new life symbolized in the coming of Jesus. In his *History of the Scottish People,* T. C. Smout describes the Covenanters as being perfectly convinced that they represented "the New Israel" and that their reformed church was the only true "bride of Christ." [13]

The Covenant tradition in southwest Scotland took several forms in terms of gatherings and ideology. It was in this region that the famous "field preachings" of the 1700s originated and grew. These local intercongregational meetings were held outdoors in the old Celtic tradition of a sacred grove. They included all the elements of kinship and religious feasting, praying, and matchmaking that persist in the later days of Piedmont Presbyterianism. Robert Burns has captured the essence of the outdoor meeting in his poem "The Holy Fair."

Burns writes with tongue in cheek of the questionable motives of the pious folk of Mauchline (whose tent, the editor tells us, was pitched so that the back entrance gave access to Nanse Tinnock's tavern, where the supplementary activities of visiting and drinking took place while the services were in progress). In the tavern and the adjoining meadows he notes the "lads an' lasses, blythely bent/ To mind baith saul an' body...." [14] The event Burns describes was held in conjunction with the Sacrament, or the Communion, which at this time was observed on the second Sunday in August, when the weather is clear and the "crops are laid by." Other popular annual Communion times are in May "after the roads are passable" and in October "before the winter sets in."

The tradition of the field preaching in connection with Communion gained power throughout Lowland Scotland, into Yorkshire and Northumbria, and over into Ulster. It is not surprising that early frontier camp meetings of the Methodists and tent revivals of the Baptists were fostered and peopled by the great hordes of Scotch-Irish and North English descendants who poured into America in the following century.

In the present-day Church of Scotland the main kin-based local congregational event continues to be the annual gathering for the Communion, during which time all the sons and daughters of the congregation return home to take part in visiting, eating, and religious celebration. Annual communion is rooted historically in the need for each church to keep records of all communicants to turn in to the General Assembly of the Church of Scotland. Every person is considered a member who takes communion once a year, regardless of his or her weekly round of participation. In order to partake of the communion elements, each communicant member must be examined by the Kirk Session on his or her doctrinal and behavioral piety. Those who "pass" (generally all members) are given a communion token which is presented at the service as an entrance ticket. Anyone not having such a ticket is not allowed to partake the elements but may sit as a visitor.

The in-group formed by all communicants of one congregation is a nuclear expression of the larger in-group of all those united together by having received the Covenant of Grace. In fact, the Covenanters themselves took communion in the sacred groves to cement their commitment to the cause.

The Southern Presbyterians of today have brought with them from their Scottish past these same practices and loyalties to their in-group of related congregations. The Covenant idea expresses the feeling of solidarity and community in which the whole congregation receives the Grace of God together—not individually. Individual conversion experiences are played down, and the emphasis is instead on the *children of* the Covenant and the *children of* Grace, born into a long line of holy and pious people who have been primary recipients of God's love.

This fusion of family, ancestors, and the handing down of the Covenant is evident in the titles of Sunday school curriculum materials and in the formal rhetoric used at ceremonies. The overall label for materials is "The Covenant Life Curriculum," which includes books entitled *The Family of Faith, Claiming the Inheritance, The Book of God's People,* and, for young couples, one called *Families Within the Family.*

The local congregation is the embodiment of the Covenant people, and the events of an individual life are also congregational events. When an infant is baptized, he or she is called by name and then "child of the Covenant." Those who are born to Presbyterian families are said to be recipients of the Covenant of Grace, and the baptismal ceremony is held within the Sunday morning worship service so that all members can publicly agree to assist the parents in rearing this child in the ways of the church. In this way all members of the congregation stand as godparents and are responsible for the child's religious growth. At a wedding, the entire congregation is viewed as a corporate witness and as a corporate support. A common prayer for newlyweds calls them "heirs to the Grace of life" and asks for their protection from the temptations of the world outside the church. Funerals are also congregational events, and the proper burial begins with a service in the church where hymns and psalms eulogize both the dead person and his or her connections to the life of the greater past and future church. The highest compliment is that a person lived "a Godly life" and "walked in the footsteps of the saints who have gone before."

The saints are also known as the priesthood of believers, part of the living Body of Christ, alive and well in the church. The saints who have gone before and the living members of the community are all joined together in a long line through which "the water of life flows, with each link in the pipeline being a Christian." The old are revered in this ethnic community because of their long association with the church on earth and because of their closeness to the church in heaven.

In relation to the rest of the world, the Covenant community stands together as passengers in a lifeboat afloat on the seas of a sinful world. In one sermon a group of people were found in a lifeboat with one uncooperative and selfish individual driving a hole in the boat, saying, "I can do this because the hole is under *my* seat!" The church, of course, will sink unless all the communicants pull together and operate as a corporate entity. In another illustration the church is a big ship that has gotten so elaborate and preoccupied with frivolous activities that it is doomed to disaster like the *Titanic.* The acceptable metaphor is that of the community of believers afloat in a small craft as if they alone are survivors of a shipwreck. I have often referred to Montreat as the "lifeboat community" because it cradles and sustains this remnant people.

In his history of an early Presbyterian congregation, that of Rocky River Presbyterian Church in North Carolina, Thomas H. Spence describes a May Meeting and dinner-on-the-grounds as the embodiment of the Covenant and kin so dear to this tradition. The description could apply equally well to a family picnic, a graveyard reunion, a Scottish communion in the Southwest of the seventeenth century, or to the summer-long gathering at Montreat.

The May Meeting not only reflects the joy of the treasured feasts of Israel, but stands as an earnest of that uninterrupted gathering around the Father's table, when the saints of all ages shall drink anew of the fruit of the vine in the blessed Kingdom of their Redeemer. It is not only a backward look to the days of Alexander Craighead, John Makemie Wilson and Daniel Lindley . . . but a prospect of the time when they, and those who follow them across the intervening years, shall assemble in the house not made with hands, at the end of the age, beside the waters of another River, which flow forever by the throne of God.[15]

Summary and Conclusion

In this article, I have attempted to illustrate the manner in which gathering patterns and important ceremonial events over time have served to forge a continuity of tradition and social structural isolation among the Southern Presbyterians. By providing a locus of value and belief reinforcement, the kin, family, and congregational regroupings serve as rites of group solidarity to rehabituate the participants and enable the culture to persist among a scattered people.

The model used here of a scattered-and-gathered community is especially useful in a highly mobile society such as ours as a means of identifying the community of cultural significance. My technique of watching *where* people go *when* and *what for* resembles the methods of natural history scientists like Archie Carr[16] who have developed means of tagging baby sea turtles and then turning them loose. When the adult turtles are picked up by a fisherman, the fisherman finds the tag requesting that the finder return it to the research base with information on the location of the find. A giant-sized map is then constructed with a pin for each location. Over time and space this gives a good picture of sea turtle movement and migration. I have attempted to chart the annual migration patterns of human groups in like manner. The annual rhythmical dispersal and assemblage of a people is always a way of defining their social-cultural meaning network.

Montreat is not an isolated example. It is not a cultural backwater left behind in the great march toward "progress" or "secularization." Instead, it stands as one example of a typical pattern within Protestant America of sacred communities that form and re-form every summer to share values and transmit culture. The Methodists have Lake Junaluska in the South and Ocean Grove, New Jersey, in the Northeast; the Baptists have Ridgecrest and other scattered conference centers; the Lutherans, Luddington, Michigan; the Quakers, Cape May, New Jersey. And for the religious but interdenominational upper middle class there is always Chautauqua; Northfield, Massachusetts; and numerous retreats in the Poconos, in the Adirondacks, and at the shore. In addition, regional camps and conferences in the woods abound, where sacred symbols are yearly recalled and young people sent back to cities to live more holy lives.

Within each one—including the upper-class nonreligious summer communities such as Hyannis Port and Martha's Vineyard or those on Long Island—the sacred cultural themes are enacted in symbolic behaviors and children relearn their expected role as adults.

Within religiously based summer communities such as the one presented here, the event itself repeated over and over serves to drive a deep shaft into the collective memory, bringing back all the revered sacred meanings common to that culture, to that particular *ethnos,* or ethnic community.[17] And in this way a group preserves and transmits its heritage through a transgenerational communal life.

John Comments

Gwen's essay on Montreat is particularly stimulating to me as a religious educator. But it raises a number of haunting questions. Obviously, religious communities and the life-styles of those communities are important for religious socialization. A great number of communities such as Montreat still exist, though some have passed away. Perhaps we ought consciously to form new ones. Living in a pluralistic world makes it difficult to maintain particular understandings and ways of life. Mindful community-building and life may be the only way Christians in the future can sustain and transmit their faith.

But before we too quickly accept such a proposition, it might be well for us to think seriously about the nature of a community. In that regard, I believe Conrad Arensberg and Solon Kimball's book *Culture and Community* [18] is of special importance. Arensberg and Kimball suggest that communities are basic units of organization within every society. As such, they have particular characteristics. The first characteristic which they identify is this: A community is composed of at least three generations and two sexes. That ought to be obvious. Surely no group can perpetuate its life without those characteristics. But it seems as if we often forget it. While local congregations typically have both sexes, they increasingly lack the integrative activity of three generations. Many of our suburban towns and their churches lack one generation, or, if they are fortunate enough to have three, their lives for all intents and purposes are separated from each other. In like manner, they often separate the activities of men and women. I have sometimes wondered if this absence of inter-generational shared life among three generations and two sexes explains why a sense of community is so often lacking in many suburban churches. Could it be that we will never regain a sense of community, no matter how much we strive for it, until we correct this situation?

A second characteristic of community mentioned by Arensberg and Kimball is the need for all the roles and statuses to be present which a group believes are essential to their understanding and way of life. Too often the church lacks some particular role, such as teacher, prophet, priest, mystic, or social activist. Perhaps we ought to establish which roles are essential for Christian community in terms of the diversity of gifts referred to by Paul. When we do, we realize that the church will have difficulty in being a community if it strives to have or to make everyone in the church be like everyone else. Without a full diversity of roles and statuses it may well be that the community of Christian faith cannot pass on its heritage or perpetuate its life. We may also conclude that a single congregation cannot possibly be a community. Perhaps only as we join together in special ways with others for life and action can we realize that sort of community essential to sustaining and transmitting Christian faith.

My continuing haunting question, however, is this: Can we make local churches into religious communities which transmit Christian faith? For one thing, it seems to me that such communities demand a variety of socioeconomic classes, races, ethnic groups, and nationalities. Yet most often churches are made up of a single class or race. How can churches expect to become Christian communities if they maintain this separateness?

Perhaps it may prove impossible to make local congregations into truly Christian communities. If so, summer religious communities which combine persons from diverse congregations and which therefore can possess the characteristics of true Christian community may be our only hope.

At any rate, I continue to struggle with the nature of community and the problems it suggests for intentional religious socialization. One thing seems clearer than ever: We need to consider seriously the structure, organization, composition, and life of the communities in which we live. And those concerns have not traditionally been in the forefront of our thinking and planning for religious education.

Of course, that's easier said than done. Radical changes have been occurring in the lives of some Christians. We are confused about our own experiences and the demands they place upon us to formulate new educational ministries that are relevant to our lives. That's the subject of my next essay.

Chapter 4

Religious Education for the Maypole Dancers [1]

John H. Westerhoff III

Reading the signs of the times is a popular endeavor, anticipating the future a current preoccupation. However, I'm neither sage nor seer, only one who, in these unsettled, confused days, is concerned for what has been variously named religious, Christian, and church education. And in this essay, I'd like to explore a few personal reflections and their implications.

The Situation

This century's middle decades were typically described as "post" something else. There were the postindustrial society and the post-Christian era, to name two. It seemed as if most of us who taught and wrote shared the perception of living in a historical interlude. An old era had ended (though it lingered on), while the shape of a new age had not quite emerged. There was a lot of talk about living between the times. Some gloried in this message. Others nostalgically regretted it. But most of us wrote as outsiders, objectively characterizing a situation which had not yet affected us personally—or so it appeared.

Then almost overnight our message changed. It was as if those post-something-else years had closed in on us. With one voice we seemed to join the ever-popular rhetoric of the day. No longer were we living in a time of slow evolutionary change; instead, we lived in the age of crisis. We announced that a radical turning point in our history—a critical time, a decisive moment from which we would either recover or die—had arrived. You can all name the crises. They are legion.

Typically, religious educators in main-line Protestant churches, in their denominational bureaucracies, and in the ecumenical seminaries uncritically parroted the radical change-post-crisis jargon of the religious scene's best-selling commentators. For a while we spoke of the "post" Sunday school era. More recently we announced the "crisis" in church education, words which correspond to the "crisis" in faith and "crisis" in the local church which others of our colleagues had announced.

Such language is understandable. Post-crisis changing times clearly express our personal experience. But the more important question is: Does it describe the overall religious situation in America? Wisely, a few cautious voices, such as Robert Lynn's of Union Theological Seminary, have pressed for a more comprehensive look at Protestant religion, the church, and education. To make such an investigation is to discover that the Sunday school is neither dead nor passé but has in fact outlived its critics and remained intact despite its reformers. As in days gone by, the Sunday school continues to be a live, healthy institution serving well America's growing evangelical conservative churches. For the vast majority of Protestants, this is neither the "post-Sunday school era" nor the "age of crisis" in Christian education. (Nor, I might add, in faith or the local church.)

In *The Big Little School,* Lynn and Wright wrote:

From the vantage point of the Time-Life building or the lofty professionalism of the seminaries, it has been easy to overlook the Sunday school as the incarnation of popular Protestantism. It [still] gives millions of youngsters some sense of how Protestants think, feel, act and sing.[2]

Now, such a newly discovered awareness does not diminish the sense of crisis many in the church experience. But it does help me to understand better the very blurred, distorted picture of what's happening within American religion and culture.

Continuity and Change

My present position, therefore, grows out of a renewed awareness of the consistency and orderliness that underlies even our modern change-conscious world. Both change and persistence are built into the unfolding order of life. Too easily we forget the conserving, persistent strength and pull of tradition. Cultural change is at best gradual. Continuity dominates history. Typically, humans strive to retain a continuous orderly tradition which will support their lives and which they can pass on to their children. Most often they succeed.

In the chapter which preceded this, Gwen examined the Southern Presbyterian summer community at Montreat, North Carolina.[3] Separated from the outside world, this denominational religious conference center composed of family cottages has persisted since 1907 as the annual gathering spot for Presbyterians of Scotch-Irish descent. This summer community is the locus for those annual rites of intensification which serve to forge ties of cultural awareness, revitalize kin relationships, introduce young people to appropriate marriage partners, guide youth to church-related educational institutions, ceremoniously restate the values and beliefs of Calvinistic Presbyterians, and provide a means for transmitting a cultural heritage to the young.

During the fall, winter, and spring these folk live in towns and cities scattered over the Piedmont South. Rarely do they come together. Due to the invisibility of their communal life, they have often been classified as "assimilated" into some sort of a general American culture. But, as Gwen contends, it is erroneous to classify this ethnic group as having been absorbed into "the American way." Their successful participation in urban life, their residence in scattered nuclear families, and even their spotty participation in the life of the church during the winter months— all this obscures the presence and persistence of ethnic and religious identity.

One of the problems faced by anyone who attempts to describe American life is the difficult task of identifying the boundaries of "a culture" or "a community" within our complex industrial society. Urban America is a melee of subcultures and overlapping communities. Yet it continues to remain true that to understand persons is to locate their "meaningful communities"—the social networks of interrelated persons which share a world view and a learned culture.

Charles Anderson has adequately defended the thesis that all of us have our roots in some ethnic group, in a people of a particular geographical, racial, religious, and national origin.

Such groups share a world view and value system; they form communities and gather for those rites, rituals, and ceremonials which support their "peoplehood."[4]

For too long we have ignored the importance of ethnicity and the dominant persistency within the numerous and diverse sub-cultures which make up our nation. America, wrote Milton Gordon, is "a mosaic of ethnic groups based upon race, religion, and to a declining extent national origin, crisscrossed by social class stratification to form characteristic subsocietal units."[5]

Witness the current resurgence of ethnic pride in American life. Consider the immense popularity of the CBS television series *All in the Family* and other similar programs. Obviously, it is not ethnicity but ethnic consciousness which is undergoing a revival. Ethnicity, as a salient factor in the American social structure, never disappeared. America has not been a great "melting pot." At best, we witness cultural borrowing—Jews patronize Chinese restaurants and pizza becomes a mainstay of the Anglo-Protestant diet. You simply cannot make a case for radical cultural change by pointing out that Wall Street bankers have long hair and beards. Ethnic and religious persistency continues to characterize American society. Change is not as dominant as we might presume, crises not as all-encompassing as they appear.

In my view, neither American culture nor religion is changing as radically or rapidly as our popular social analyzers would have us suppose. In the realm of simple observation and common sense, nothing is more obvious than the conservative bent of human behavior, the manifest desire to preserve, hold, fix, and keep stable.

It is important to remember that, while cultural change is as historically real as stability, continuity is most normal. As Robert Nisbet wrote:

One need but look at the actual history of any given way of behavior in a group or society—the way of behavior we call the monogamous family in the West, for example, or the Christian church, or the university—and while changes in these are indeed aspects of the historical record, such changes can only be understood against the background of persistence that must, if we are to understand change, be our point of departure.[6]

To be sure, most main-line Protestant denominations (the COCU churches and others like them) are struggling to survive what they hope will be a temporary adversity. While there is no evidence that they are dying, they are surely diminishing in size. Typically, there is tension between those who wish to conserve and those who desire change. At the same time those denominations which support and reinforce the most conserving aspect of American culture and its ethnic subsocietal grouping—the Southern Baptist Convention, the Pentecostal and Holiness groups, the Evangelicals, the Mormons, Jehovah's Witnesses, Seventh-Day Adventists, and many smaller groups hardly visible to the large denominations—exhibit stability and growth.[7]

For corresponding reasons the increasing strength and vitality of the black church corresponds with a simultaneous resurgence of black consciousness and the birth of black theology.[8] Likewise, certain religious groups have always been dominant among particular ethnic groups. By the same token, we can explain why people from distinct geographical areas and national origins express faith in particular ways. My point is this: Religion and culture are intimately bound together. Where a subculture and its ethnic group have consciousness, stability, and vitality, there religion tends to be stable and vital also. This situation should help us understand why the crises in the church, faith, and church education not only go together but tend to be limited to particular subcultural groups and their members.

Culture implies a common way of life, a common understanding of life, and a common set of values. Religion is intimately bound to culture. It expresses a people's way of life, it gives their lives meaning, and it provides them with understanding. In complex cultures, religious institutions assume these sustaining and supporting functions. Insofar as they satisfactorily perform such roles, religious institutions are participated in and supported. When they no longer perform these functions well, they face a crisis. When there is disruption in culture, there is disruption in religion and vice versa.

It is within this context that I think we can begin to understand what many white Anglo-Saxon ethnics and the main-line Protestant churches are living through. Let me try to describe what I think is happening.

An Analysis

In teaching her introductory class in cultural anthropology, Gwen constructs a three-dimensional map of the United States, blocking off geographical regions, setting off distinct communities of ethnic, religious, racial, and national origin, and dividing each into stratified layers according to socioeconomic class. Most people could be placed somewhere on that map. For a majority of the population, much of the popular literature on rapid change, religion, and culture is to a major extent meaningless, irrelevant, and indeed not at all applicable. Persistency rather than change dominates their lives. Stability rather than crisis best describes their experience. A traditional world view and value system and the institutions (including the church and even its Sunday school) which support them are essentially secure and meaningful.

However, having attempted to fit everyone into a place on our map, we discover a group of people who do not seem to fit. They tend to be the same group for whom the rhetoric of post-crisis radically changing times is real. Most social analyzers are among them. Many could be classified as "intellectuals," though not all. The one factor they have in common is their loss of a sense of "peoplehood." They sometimes describe a conscious striving to express a world view that makes sense of their experience, or to establish a set of values by which they might live, or to find a purposeful community with rituals and ceremonies which will support their understanding of life. But most often they just seem to feel without a home, without a supportive community, without a way to express their faith or pass it on to their children. For them, the old forms *are* passing, a crisis *does* exist.

In order to fit these people onto her neat little map, Gwen found it necessary to construct a "maypole" on top, linking all those who are unattached to set groups and cultures. She called these people the "maypole dancers." These maypole dancers are among a growing number of persons in American culture who have been jarred by experience and their reflections out of their subcultural homes and have become estranged from their ethnic group. They find themselves like dancers around a maypole, celebrating their newly discovered freedom and their commitment to cultural change but painfully hoping that somehow a new pattern of life, meaning, and community will emerge so they can stop their frantic dancing.

Perhaps many of you who will read this essay are, to one extent or another, among these maypole dancers. Insofar as you are, you are among that growing number of folk who just aren't sure about their faith or their life. In many ways you seem to be out of step with your people of origin. Sometimes you are estranged from your own families, or at least from the communities in which you were raised and the early peer groups which once claimed your allegiance. The world looks different to you. You don't share any longer the same perceptions about the nature of life and the meaning of history. You appear to possess a different consciousness from many of those who in other ways are like you. But you are still not clear what that consciousness is or how to express it. Your values most likely disagree with the majority of persons who make up American society; perhaps you even disagree with your own family's, if not in theory at least in practice. Also your life-style is probably at variance with the masses. Some of you experience your most frustrating times in church—that is, if you still are active. Here you expect to have your faith and values nourished and nurtured. Instead you find yourself in conflict. Occasionally you drop out. Yet that doesn't seem to bring contentment. At other times, you strive to make the church and its life correspond to your way of seeing things. Frustration often ensues, as you discover that few others share your desires.

Many of the church's rites and rituals lack reality for you; the church's life rings untrue, its actions devoid of significance. You desire change in both church and culture. You have a vision of a different society and a different expression of religion. You may claim Christian faith, but you have difficulty finding a community which shares your perceptions and supports your way of life. Only one thing you know for sure—you can't go home again.

Obviously, I'm describing a particular class of maypole dancer. There are others. The diversity is great. Yet all have in common what might be described as a socially deviant world view, value system, and life-style. All in their own ways are searching for personal styles and institutional forms which express their view of life. All, to some extent, are estranged from their subcultural ethnic group of origin and cannot yet find another community to call home. Their anxieties over faith and life are closely related to this lostness from a people, their own community, among whom they can say "I feel at home."

It's not easy to know why anyone becomes a maypole dancer, but there seem to be numerous common characteristics. While some were brought up within or on the fringe of liberal main-line religious institutions and others within typically conservative religious groups, almost all of them have married outside of their family's religious and ethnic group or have lived in intimate relationships with those who are different from their people of origin. In their homes (or in their churches, schools, or peer groups), they were most often influenced by the conviction that no one has a monopoly on truth and that all insights should be examined objectively. Taught that openness and dialogue were good, they came to appreciate individual differences and the importance of the unprejudiced sharing of insights. Typically, they traveled or moved a good deal. However, the one most prevalent characteristic is this: Maypole dancers have had numerous radical and significantly different experiences from those persons who rarely get outside the influence of their own environment of origin with its supporting kin and peer groups.

While small in numbers, the importance of the maypole dancers cannot be ignored. Insofar as cultural change is occurring, the maypole dancers are part of that change. The character of religion and the role it will play in such an emerging culture could, therefore, likewise be at least partially in their hands. As other maypole dancers before them, they may be an important indicator group in the movement of cultural and religious change. So it is that they can also abort and become another forgotten group in the history of religion and culture. Yet to understand them is to catch a glimpse of one conceivable tomorrow. To act with them is to encourage and make possible an alternative future. Their strivings will vary, but religion will be central to both their quest and goal. So will education.

Significance of Religion

I say that, because I believe all of us are incorrigibly religious —that is, we demand an understanding of life. Religion, with its communities, rituals, and ceremonies, symbolically answers this need by communicating, reinforcing, and providing a context for the development of a personal world view and value system.

Education provides the means by which we consciously strive to reinforce that meaning in our lives as well as pass it on to our young. Culture is kept alive by this twofold transmission of shared meaning; it continually nourishes and nurtures persons.

We are born as human persons or selves with a need to make sense of the world and to find a meaningful place for ourselves within it. Religious socialization (as I have defined it) is the name for the process by which we interact with others and develop a personal faith and way of life; it is an interactive enterprise by which we discover meaning and acquire values.

Traditionally, persons have participated in this interactive process of "meaning-making" within the context of historical social forms of religion, forms closely bound to the culture. That is, faith has been mediated through and reconstructed within the institutions of a culture—in the more complex societies of the West, through special differentiated institutions, such as the church. Thus, it is through and within such social structures that persons acquire, sustain, and communicate their faith and values. Insofar as these institutions satisfactorily perform these functions, persons seek them out and participate in their life.

But here lies one of the problems faced by the maypole dancers. For them, life in the old communities no longer makes sense or inspires their lives. They search for new or reformed religious institutions.

A significant number of our maypole dancers have lost an identifiable, supportive community of shared meaning, a people which expresses in personally significant ways a common faith and encourages life-styles consistent with that faith. For them a new faith community needs to be discovered or created. Meaningful rites and rituals, myths and symbols, expressions of beliefs, organizational patterns, activities, and experiences need to emerge. For them an alternative to the present programs in religious education is essential. It is to that problem I'd like to turn.

The Nature of Education

First: a few words on the nature of education. Too many of us, including educators, are guilty, as I pointed out in an earlier essay, of a too-narrow conception of education. We view education as something which results from attending school. Thus, experiences which occur outside of school become nonsanctioned learnings, not to be taken seriously when planning for education. Yet most of us will admit that our most significant learning took place outside of school. We know that education and schooling are not synonymous, but we behave as if they were.

Dwayne Huebner of Teachers College, Columbia,[9] recently asked: Why does the church put the young in classrooms with their peers and a teacher to be instructed in ways modeled after secular education? Is it because we do not know how to be with them in religious ways? Because it is easier to try to teach children what to think, instruct them in what to feel, and tell them how to believe than to be with them and share with them that which is ours, that upon which we live our lives and find our meaning? Isn't living religiously with others inherently educational? If we focus on being religious with others, need we attend to schooling? What does it mean to be together religiously? What does it mean to be a community of faith?

Such questions raise to high visibility the concern I have named "religious socialization," or that comprehensive social process by which persons acquire and sustain their faith and life-style. It is my contention that this process must become the primary concern of the maypole dancers if they are to find a home in the world, acquire a new sense of peoplehood, and learn the means for transmitting their new understanding and way of life to their children.

The Goal of Religious Socialization

However, even if we agree on the importance of socialization, we face a more pressing question: Toward what end are our socializing efforts to be addressed? Too often we become preoccupied with means. It would be foolish to neglect the difficult quest for ends. Of course, only after we have unified means and ends have we been mindful. Nevertheless we need to ask the question: For what purposes do we intend to plan for intentional religious socialization? My answer is this: The goal of religious socialization is the transmission and support of a particular faith and life-style, for example (from my personal perspective), one described by the adjective Christian.[10]

When I speak of this particularity as Christian, I point toward a view or understanding of the world, our place in it, and the behavioral guides by which we make our decisions. For me, that means an understanding of the world as ordered and purposeful, moving in an intentional direction.[11] It assumes that in a particular historical activity—the Christ event—a clear vision of its directionality and a call to participate in historical actions which will contribute to its fulfillment are revealed. But more about that in another chapter.

The term life-style points toward faith's individual and corporate expressions. Each of us is a thinking, feeling, willing self. It is our way of life, our total behavior in every moment of time, which gives expression to our faith. As such, for a Christian maypole dancer, Christian faith as personally grasped and its corresponding life-style as corporately lived are the primary goals of religious socialization.

The Means of Religious Education

For the maypole dancer who affirms the task and goals we've described, three primary means of intentional religious socialization or religious education emerge:[12]

First, to create meaningful ceremonials (rites and rituals) which embody one's faith and support and transmit its meaning and vision.

Second, to establish opportunities for the community of shared meaning to experience and reflect upon its faith and thereby evolve an integrated set of answers to questions about oneself and the world.

And third, to provide opportunities for planned action around those personal and social issues which emerge from a desire to actualize one's faith and live out one's values.

We'll examine each of these briefly.

Ritual

Religious education requires meaningful celebrations of faith. In the article that follows this one, Gwen Neville deals with the meaning and function of rituals. Let me say briefly that the ritual celebrations of a faith community act to sustain their particular way of looking at the world and their understanding of a way of life. Rituals provide both the form and the occasion for the expression of faith. From the viewpoint of theology, it is through our participation in ritual action, movement, song, dance, and storytelling that we become aware of the meaning and value of life, our reason for living, and our motives for acting.

Where better can the myths, symbols, folk tales, and sacred stories which undergird and express faith be meaningfully communicated? How better can we pass on our world view than in the ceremonial life of "our" people? What better means is there for the maintenance of historical consciousness?

As an example of the way ritual in one culture restates a world view, Dorothy Lee points to the Dakota Indians.[13] The Dakotas affirm the relatedness, the universal oneness, and the ultimate unity of all things. They therefore created a series of rites which communicate and reinforce that world view by encouraging absolute humility and the complete abandonment of self. During a deeply religious ceremonial, the holy man who sponsors a lamenter prays, "Our grandmother and mother [earth], this man wishes to become one with all things . . . for the good of all our people help him." The lamenter then climbs alone to a selected spot on a mountain where, exposed to danger and the elements, naked and fasting, he empties himself, striving for a vision of oneness and praying, "O wakan-Tanka, have pity on me that my people may live." The individual is made one with the elements, and through his actions the community is revived.

One of the problems of the maypole dancers is the difficulty of finding a group that can agree on a faith to restate symbolically, even if they could agree on a time and place to assemble! At a recent workshop on "rituals and ceremonies for the church of the future," a group of participants could agree on only one belief that they all shared, and that was a belief in change. So as their group presentation they created a ritual celebrating change. A priority task for the maypole dancers is to discover and unite in celebrations of their faith.

Experience

The second requirement of religious education is experience consistent with a people's faith and life-style. Modes of feeling, thinking, and acting are passed on from one generation to another through experience in a social context. Faith is fostered and evolved within that community which takes experience seriously.

As we pointed out earlier, the world view of the Dakotas affirms being one with all and responsible for all. Experience plays a major role in passing on this understanding. The Dakotas were taught that to serve the tribe was to serve oneself. This coextensiveness of self and society was communicated and reinforced through particular experiences. For example, when a boy killed his first bird, his father celebrated the event by giving away a horse to an old man who could not return the gift. Such experiences were considered to be "religious education."

In like manner, if a mother and father decide that their interests and needs are more important than their child's, they are apt to feed the baby on a convenient schedule with a bottle held by some mechanical device. This baby is just as well nourished as one breast-fed on demand but will grow up with a different, perhaps more individualistic and self-centered, outlook.

Thus experience plays an important role in the framing, development, and sustenance of faith and life.

Every act or experience means something particular to each person. What it means is, in part, a result of previous experiences. To share experience with meaningful others is the way by which we frame our way of looking at life.

When the meaning of numerous acts, experiences, and events are put together, consciously or unconsciously, in an overall view of life, we have the world view out of which we act and reflect on all future acts and experiences. Experience, therefore, is a key to both the formation and expression of our faith.

Another way of stating this is to say that faith cannot be communicated without experiences consistent with that faith. For example, persons may be taught the thirty-nine articles or whatever, but if they never experience others who express reverence for a power directing the course of history, they will have difficulty acquiring a faith that affirms an understanding of the world as ordered, purposeful, and moving in an intentional direction. Recall that Carlisle has one of his characters express his own reflected-upon understanding of religious growth with these words: "The highest whom I knew on earth, I here saw bowed down, with awe unspeakable, before a highest in heaven; such things especially in infancy, reach without words to the very core of your being."

Living faith demands experience. A recovery—or perhaps, better, a rediscovery—of religious experience is a primary responsibility of a community of faith. For too long we have distrusted the feelings and missed the depths of life's meaning. We have ignored the ordinary experiences of life, missed meaning's heart and the experiential forms and contents of faith. The faith community needs to reemphasize the importance of religious experience in its life and the lives of its members.

But experience all by itself will not suffice. In these days of a partial rebirth of concern for experience, it is too easy to neglect or deprecate the intellectual or reflective dimensions of life.

A person feels, acts, and thinks. We each need to make sense of our experience. Through the use of our intellect, we gain and give expression to our overarching interpretation of life. We need to interpret and explicate faith—that is, we need to be able to express an interpretive set of beliefs about ourselves and the world in which we live. We need to evolve through reflected-upon experience an integrated set of answers to our questions about ourselves and the world. Thus it is that the maypole dancers will have to take seriously experiential religion as well as provide opportunities for sharing intellectual reflection and expression.

Action

The third and last requirement of religious education is planned action as an expression of faith. We all spend our lives in a complex web of direct and indirect social interaction. "Religion is not so much theology as life. It is to be lived rather than reasoned about," wrote James Pratt.[14] Surely, we must act out our faith before we can fully comprehend it. Education requires activism. Religion is not only rational and mystical, it is also practical or moral—that is, it lays emphasis on things done as well as believed and felt.

The communication of faith requires opportunities for appropriate action on behalf of the learner. Just as we cannot learn what we do not experience, we cannot learn what we have not acted upon. Faith without works is most certainly dead. We can teach a set of literal beliefs by verbal instruction, but we cannot evolve a living faith. Faith cannot come alive in a person apart from its conceptualization in moments of significant action.

Faith cannot be our faith if we only talk about it. We therefore need to provide a place where children, young people, and adults together consciously and overtly attempt to translate faith into action. For every belief we profess, an opportunity must be sought to make it real in an identifiable and interpreted action.

For the Dakotas, remember, responsibility was rooted in an increased awareness of relationship. Every child was therefore given responsible work of social consequence. When he was three, for example, a boy might be asked to bring his father's pony to be bridled or to go from tepee to tepee to find the village whetstone. There was no supervision. The father would not repeat his request or go after the pony himself. All would have to pay the price, without criticism, of the child's behavior if that boy neglected his responsibility. But the child experiencing trust from the earliest years and having witnessed others perform these acts knew what was expected. Children who, accompanying their parents daily, are quietly reminded that someday, when they are older, they will act accordingly, learn a way of life consistent with a particular world view.

And that world view correspondingly will express itself in actions. Take, for example, the Jehovah's Witnesses. They have what might be described as a pessimistic outlook on the state of the world, the present and the future. That world view provides an explanation of evil and the chaos and complexity of life. It results in actions. Instead of getting involved in the world, striving for gain or participating in politics, they preach and witness to the end of time, that souls may be saved. Within this resulting life-style of action, they acquire the identity, roles, and status necessary for life. These actions frame a world view which, in turn, influences their actions.

Of course, participation in action alone is not enough. We need also to be concerned about what we do in preparation to act. Faithful actions are a result of decision-making; that implies learning to act and practice in acting. The faith community needs to be seen as a laboratory and training ground.

Faith can only make sense in the context of experience and participation in the life of faith. A life-style can only be learned through radical experiments in action. The actual and everyday life of the community of faith is to be at the heart of its educational methodology. And the maypole dancers will need to understand that "the life of their community" needs to express deliberate purposefulness in concrete personal and social actions, consistent with their faith.

Conclusion

Faith—a meaningful story of the world and our place in it—is communicated by and within an intentional community, by a people and their historical existence. Such a community of people will continually strive to order their lives—their ceremonials, experiences, and actions—in ways consistent with their faith. Education is the purposeful, intentional ways that this community of faith provides rites and rituals to sustain and nurture its faith, a context for experience and reflection on experience of the meaning and purpose of life and for participation in actions aimed at the actualization of their values. The maypole dancers will need to explore their understandings of life and desired ways of life. They will need to join with others who share their beliefs, attitudes, values, and behaviors to form intentional communities of shared meanings and ways. And as part of this process, they will need to plan intentional forms of religious socialization combining ceremonials, experience, and action so that they may both sustain their own life and pass it on to their children.

But all that is, of course, still theoretical and general. I have not dictated clearly or precisely what the maypole dancers must do. I make no apology for that. In days of unsettledness and change, when people are apt to grasp at any practical suggestion, a sound foundational base is more essential. In this essay, I have only attempted to provide a basis for an understanding of our contemporary situation and a theoretical model for religious education among the maypole dancers—namely, a socialization model which provides the basis for an alternative future for education in the church.

However, before I end these reflections, I would remind us all who have become maypole dancers and are attracted by Christian faith that Abraham, the man and archetype of faith, was a wanderer. God's constant word to him was to leave the familiar and secure with only a promise that was to be fulfilled in the future. What Abraham had to believe was that God lived in the tents of wandering pilgrims. The problem came when Abraham's people were no longer on a journey, when they believed they had arrived. Gail Deason, a friend of mine and onetime staff member at the American Church in Paris, puts it this way:

Remember when the rushing stream of Israel's history had become a land-locked lake. It was then that the Prophets thundered against her self-deception with the news that God was about to move out in a new direction. And He would deal with all the established institutions, even his holy ones, if they proved intransigent and unwilling to move. So the prophets called for a breaking of the dam so that the river of Israel's dynamic faith could flow once more.

I for one take confidence and hope from this tradition, a tradition which states that the will of God is a promised future. From this forward gaze can come the momentum for hopeful wandering. As maypole dancers we know that we are unable to live in the stability of things as they are. We find ourselves as wanderers, called to go forth. As a pilgrim people, we know not where we are headed or exactly which road lies ahead. Yet, willing to wander forth in faith, we will perhaps become the unworthy, unprepared people of God for tomorrow.

That brings to a close my first thoughts on religious education for the maypole dancers, only a small first contribution to a complex problem. The path to solutions of such problems is long and difficult. Too many persons prefer a quick and easy route. "There are many people," wrote Kierkegaard, "who reach their conclusions about life like school boys. They cheat their master by copying the answer out of a book without working out the sum for themselves." [15] All of us are tempted to be among the seekers of easy answers. Yet we know this is no solution to our needs. In the light of those needs, may this rambling first exploration into an alternative future for education in the church have some relevance and even the seeds necessary for a shared adventure.

Gwen Comments

I really like the imagery of the maypole dancers as those who are seeking new kinds of communities and new life-styles—and not just because I first dreamed it up. It makes a good addendum to an otherwise stratified, set, and explainable religious system. I like it because it always seems to fit and to ring a bell when I try it out on those who have cut loose from traditional moorings. And I like it because it portrays these seekers not as fragmented, neurotic, and lost but simply as tied with longer ribbons to new center stakes for their community of faith.

Several sociologists have defined these groups of seekers and have attempted to describe their component populations. Milton Gordon, to whom John also refers, developed early theories on group life and its expressions, and his students Anderson and Murray [16] have expanded the quest for explanatory and descriptive data on the white Protestants and on the university intellectual elite. Berger refers to these intellectuals who share a world view based on science or philosophy as "cognitive minorities." [17] My own research has been directed at the double goals of describing the continuing group life of a religious culture and at the same time seeking to identify and explain what happens to the ones who choose to drop out.

The group I studied, reported partially in a previous chapter, is a classic example of an internal segment of what John calls "main-line Protestantism." Among my "people" a strong ethnic cultural identity has persisted through a period of over seven generations—around 250 years.

Now I have asked myself over and over: What happens to the marginal folk who are Presbyterian or Methodist or Baptist by their own declaration but who do not take part in the intensive annual religious gatherings? And, furthermore, what about the central core of celebrants—the people in the lifeboat community —when they return to their daily urban business routines? Both groups live and act out three quarters of their lives or more within the so-called "secular world," using cultural rules common to a wider group of urban dwellers who may come from multiple religions and nonreligions.

Other writers and researchers have attempted to get at this double-meaning system in American life. Robert Bellah has written about the American Civil Religion, Peter Berger about the Sacred Canopy and Thomas Luckmann about the Invisible Religion,[18] in an attempt to explain the shared systems of overarching meaning that must tie together a society built on religious pluralism.

My own way of trying to explain the existence and mechanisms of the two rule systems is based on the model of a bilingual child. This child speaks and acts in Spanish or French at home and then transfers to an all-American spoken and action language for functioning at school or, later, in the business world. The double set of meanings is enacted ritually in a private and in a public set of ritual behaviors and beliefs. Public rituals operate at an entirely different level of meaning and social integration from the home and church rituals of the private world. We need to continue to explore the way private worlds of meanings and rituals are interfaced with the world of public ceremony, school, work, science, and medicine. I have explored this double-meaning system in my chapter on ceremonies and social networks which follows.

Chapter 5

Rites and Rituals
for a Double World—
Private and Public Meanings

Gwen Kennedy Neville

"Ritual" has almost become a dirty word in the writings of
church persons on worship and on education. It has somehow
taken on the negative connotation of being a cultic leftover from
a less civilized time, and the phrase "empty ritual" has been used
in the new liberal writing to describe much of the church's traditional liturgy and orders of worship. Because of these negative
meanings, I was reluctant to use the word in this essay and
instead set out to substitute "ceremony" and "ceremonial life."
After reconsideration, however, I am convinced that rite and
ritual need to be properly redefined within the context of human
cultures and reinterpreted for the religious communities as non-
judgmental descriptive terms related not so much to theological
as to anthropological meanings.

From the viewpoint of anthropology, ritual behavior could be
defined as any behavior which is stereotyped, repetitive, and
nonobligatory.[1] In other words, almost all human activities involve
some degree of ritual behavior. Cutting down a tree might be an
obligatory behavior for survival. Ritual elaboration prescribes
that one hold the ax in a certain way or say magical words before
and after the tree is cut. Eating food is obligatory for survival.
The amount of ceremony surrounding the setting of a proper
table, pouring of wine (and the proper wine), and serving of
afterdinner coffee is ritual—but very much a part of a cultural
pattern.

Ritual, then, is culturally patterned, and ritual behaviors all together function like a language which is mutually intelligible to the speakers but not to nonspeakers. There is an "expectedness" among co-members who agree on shared language. They can pick up subtle behavior signals from one another—such as when it is time to leave a party or when to sit, stand, and kneel at church. Ritual language is so strong and so communicative because it is stereotyped. It is repetitive. The same situation produces exactly the same behavior over and over again.[2]

Even though we find ritual behavioral language in the normal secular events of life, we find the most stylized and most persistent ritual associated with sacred events. These include weekly worship services, prayer, and sacred ceremonies surrounding the seasons and the life of the individual. Within these sacred rituals a form of intense telescoping takes place of the meanings and values that are most dear to that culture. These are condensed into symbols and symbolic actions that state, in a kind of sacred shorthand, the core values of the group. Durkheim calls this process "telescoping" within ritual. E. R. Leach compares it to the condensation of signals within a transistor, so it becomes a "transistorizing" of crucial elements.[3]

To assist in the telescoping process, all cultures use music, dance, unfolding drama, verbal reinforcement, and the arrangement of space as aids in communicating the desired message. Participation in the recurrent rituals, then, has a positive effect on the rededication of participants to the central cultural themes.

Examples of this patterned use of space and other elements can be found in the arrangement of the church sanctuary to express various world views. Once Roman Catholic and Episcopal churches had their altars high above the congregation and placed far behind the pulpit to symbolize the holiness and sacredness of God, with the minister or priest standing as intermediary between God and the assembled worshipers. Early Presbyterian and Baptist churches had pulpits that were placed in the center of the chancel to symbolize the centrality of the Bible and the preaching of the Word. In some nineteenth-century Methodist churches the pews were arranged in a semicircle around the chancel to communicate equality of all the saints and equal access for all to God's word.

The behavior of each group in its Sunday service is also patterned and sequenced according to cultural expectedness.

Episcopalians kneel to pray, Presbyterians sit to pray, Methodists stand to pray. Presbyterians hold dear the set order of worship, as they value order in all areas of life and thought. Episcopalians value the dramatic form and the liturgical aspects of reverence and emotion. The worship behavior sequences are a part of other aspects of the cultural form that make up a unified whole, in which the world view of each separate people is stated symbolically.

The Koinonia Farm community in Americus, Georgia, is an interesting example of a group which attempted to leave religious rites and rituals behind. However, being an agricultural community, as soon as the harvest was in they began the custom of a thanksgiving meal, which in time became ritualized. Even though they ignored a Christmas ritual, being busy with the packaging and sale of pecans, soon after Christmas they joined in a celebration of their labors. And when the first member of the community died, a ritual had to be created.[4] No community can exist without a ceremonial life. Too often we ignore that fact.

Because the rituals and ceremonials of a people are tightly patterned and stylized to restate a certain world view, these sequences are among the most rooted in individual and cultural sacredness and are among the most difficult sequences to change. The innovators who have attempted to initiate the folk mass, the contemporary worship, or the "celebration" know well the kind of strong resistance they meet. It could mean that the older forms *were* valuable and were serving a needed function in the cultural system, while the new forms are appropriate for the newer emerging culture systems that make sense to the people we have labeled maypole dancers. These simply are *not* most of the people of the churches, although they may be over-represented among the innovators.

Having established that rituals and ceremonies are necessary and positive for cultural maintenance, let us focus on the various types of ritual celebrations common to all cultures and on the functions they perform within the society.

Communal Rituals—Sacred and Secular

One of the universal types of rituals that we find in all societies is that which is celebrated periodically—weekly, monthly or yearly—by a group of people sharing a common world view. In simple societies these calendrical celebrations go along with the changes in the moon, with shifts in the hunting season, or shifts in the agricultural cycle. Biological time sequences—days, moons, seasons—are translated through ritual enactments into cultural sequences that place special meaning on the everyday aspects of food-getting and family life.

Among the Murngin, a hunting and gathering people of Australia, for example, the two basic seasons are "wet" and "dry." During the wet season little movement is possible, game is scarce, and scattered family camps live separately in order to exploit the scarce resources of the semidesert environment. As the wet season ends there is an abundance of food and wildlife, families begin to move about, and the patterns of food-getting and family structure begin to shift. As an accompaniment to this shift, a ceremonial time marks the transition. All the families in the band gather together for a joint celebration reenacting their sacred beliefs and values.[5]

This scattered-and-gathered pattern of ceremonial community is also found among the Plains tribes of North America. The Cheyenne lived in nomadic bands throughout the winter when hunting was difficult and regathered in large units for the buffalo hunt in late spring. Their great combined ceremonies are now famous. The Sun Dance united all the various bands into one great camp circle in which all tepees faced eastward to the rising sun and in which the arrangement and ordering of placement of tepees corresponded to the hierarchy of families and bands within the tribe. A similar Cheyenne ceremony, the Arrow Renewal, held in alternate years, served to renew the power of the sacred arrows which symbolically stated the tribe's good luck in hunting that had been promised them by a mythical culture hero, Sweet Medicine.[6]

Agricultural peoples have ceremonies to mark the shift from "growing time" to "harvest time" and, after the harvest, to mark a shift to the season of restful waiting before planting. We have inherited many of our own religious calendrical rituals from our agriculturally based forebears. Thanksgiving, for example, is an agricultural celebration, although 90 percent of us are now town- and city-dwellers. Other ceremonial shifts in our economic patterns include the behavioral shift from the school year into summer and back again. "Summer" in the United States has become a form of sacred time based on the institutional shift of public schools, a pattern also established in response to the agricultural economic base in which children were needed as field hands during growing season and harvest time. Now we have two ritually celebrated all-American holidays to mark this shift—Memorial Day to begin and Labor Day to close.

All group ceremonies, of course, do not mark such distinct economic shifts in activities. There are those that recur weekly as rhythmic time-keepers marching through the calendar year, revitalizing the worshipers with the experience of having restated beliefs symbolically. There are also ceremonies to mark institutional shifts in activity, such as opening convocation at colleges and closing services at revivals and conferences. These act to establish a new set of expected behaviors, or a new and changed pattern of activity for participants, as they pass through one type of activity into another. In American society we can observe at least three concurrent calendar "years" in process—that of the school, the church, and the commercial-industrial complex. Each will have its own cycles and rhythms. Each will have activity shifts marked by rituals restating periodically its own group position, beliefs, values, and world view.

Anthropologists have variously labeled these ceremonies marking calendrical and behavioral shifts. Chapple and Coon first coined the label "rites of intensification" to denote the aspect of intensifying the group commitment and reviving tired loyalties and actions.[7] Rites of intensification can include as simple a recurrent gathering as a family meal or a weekly prayer meeting. They can be as all-inclusive as the great tribal ceremonies of the Cheyenne, the sacred summer community described for the American South, or the large national civil religious gathering every four years for Presidential Inauguration. Each one serves to restate shared values and to reestablish the devotion of the believer-participant.

Because our complex society is made up of overlapping belief communities in both the personal religious sphere and in the public business arena, each person becomes a part of multiple worlds, each sharing its own special unfolding ceremonial cycle. The individual who is part of a family, a church, a school (either as student, parent, or teacher), and a business or industry will be a participant in the rites of intensification belonging to the annual cycle of each. I have attempted to illustrate this as a diagram or chart (Figure 1). The family world will vary with each nuclear unit, including the birthdays of each person, anniversaries, and traditional times for large family get-togethers and reunions. All three of the other institutional cycles share certain features that overlap and have influence on one another.

Rituals for the Individual in Transition

In addition to the large group ceremonies and rituals commemorating shifts in the institutional cycle, all cultures celebrate a second type of ritual. This type is centered on the individual and her or his life cycle rather than on the group and its continuation. The ceremonies surrounding the life cycle of individuals are found at those times when the person is in transition from one biological or social state to another.

At birth, puberty, marriage, parenthood, menopause, and death the individual is passing through changes that will affect her or his interaction with other group members. Certain behaviors are expected of a child that would not be appropriate after becoming an adult in the same culture. Many preliterate societies have elaborate puberty ceremonies to mark this transition. Where the discrepancy between appropriate roles for child and adult is greatest, the ceremony is most elaborate. It serves as an important ritual restatement of the old and the new roles the individual has played and will play within his or her world. It moves the person ceremonially into a new social position.

These types of ceremonies associated with transition were first called "rites of passage" by Arnold van Gennep in 1909, and since then they have been studied extensively by anthropologists.[8] Van Gennep noted that a transition ritual has three important phases within its unfolding structure—Separation, Transition, and Incorporation.

The early phase is that of Separation. In this phase the person is symbolically set apart from the former group of associates. An example can be seen in the ritual isolation of a new graduate who is capped and gowned to remove her or him symbolically from the other undergraduates.

In separating the graduate spatially and ceremonially, the planners have set the stage for phase II, which is the Transitional or Marginal period when the individual is neither fish nor fowl,

Figure 1
INSTITUTIONAL CYCLES IN AMERICAN SOCIETY

		School	Church	National-Civil, Commercial-Industrial
January	Winter	Exams	*Beginning of year Epiphany	*Beginning of year
February		Beginning again Basketball games Pep rallies		Lincoln's Birthday Washington's Birthday
March	Spring		Lent	
April		Spring break	Easter	Easter (spring) Clothing and candies, etc.
May		Graduation parties	Pentecost	Spring holidays Memorial Day
June	Summer	Graduation	Scatter for summer	
July		Summer vacation	Summer Camps and conferences	July 4th Summer vacations
August			"Revivals"	
September	Fall	*Beginning of year "Rush parties" Football games Pep rallies	Regathering from summer	Labor Day
October				Columbus Day Halloween
November		Thanksgiving break	Advent	Thanksgiving Day
December	Winter	Christmas break	Christmas	Christmas shopping Office parties Suburban social scene

neither student nor graduate, but only a person in the middle. (Some social observers have speculated that all of college is one long elaborate puberty ritual, moving the person from child to adult status.) Another ceremony where this transitional phase is readily observable is that of marriage. The couple enters the church separately from two different entrances. At first the bride stands at the altar on the arm of her father, between the personification of her status as a child in a family and the embodiment in the groom of her new role as the wife in another household. She is during this brief central phase of the ceremony neither girl-child nor woman-wife. She is in transition.

The third phase of the rites of passage is that of Incorporation. The graduate marches across the stage to receive the diploma, shakes hands with the college president, and changes the tassel on the graduation cap from one side to another to symbolize the beginning of the new status of "alumnus." The bride is given in marriage by her father and is incorporated into her new role when the groom takes her hand and the two stand alone before the altar and then leave as a couple together. They have come into the church single and leave married. The ceremony moves them into an entirely new social state.

In all societies the rites of passage function in two ways. One is to provide meaning, and the other is to consolidate a support group for transitional individuals. The biological life crises of birth and death are the most traumatic to the social group into which individuals come and out of which they go. Birth and death are mysteries that must be explained through a culture's belief systems and celebrated by an ideological community. The newborn infant is seen by Christians as a gift of God and is dedicated through baptism. The ceremony moves the infant ritually from the world of the nonliving into the world of social reality in which she or he is assigned meaningful place. It also moves a couple from the status of young marrieds to the all-new position of parents.

Whereas baptism serves to open up a new social field of relational possibilities and to give thanks for new life, the funeral acts to close the social vacuum that results from an individual's death. If a person has had a long and busy life among many friends and kinsmen, the void is particularly great. Of course the social emptiness is most keenly felt by the immediate family.

Funeral ritual in all cultures serves to restate meanings and values about both death and life—to honor the deceased for her or his life but also to explain and assign meaning to death within an overall plan of reality. Within the funeral as a rite of passage, the deceased person moves now from the world of the living into the world of those who have gone before, and the mystery of death is explained through the shared faith of the attending community.

Ceremonies surrounding birth, puberty, marriage, and death not only serve to assign meaning to the raw data of biological cycles but also to forge together a communal group to assist the transitional individual, providing support, assistance, and encouragement. Note that the transitional individuals include not only the dead but also the surviving kin group, not only the baby but also the parents and grandparents. In the South an old custom dictates that at a death all the friends and neighbors bring food to the house. Kin gather, visit, talk, and renew ties. Flowers are for the people left behind—a ceremonial statement of support during a crisis time. The actual funeral ritual begins at the moment of death and moves through set stages for each culture from the mourning, the gathering of kin, the service, and the burial, and does not actually end until the final disposition of property and practical arrangements for the family have been completed.

Individuals pass through transitional periods not only based on biological changes but also based on changes in social position. Graduation and marriage are essentially changes in social position. Other changes in social state result from divorce, retirement, and widowhood. Within the productive occupational life, transitions occur upon promotion, ordination for the priesthood, and other changes in status or behavior resulting from moving or changing jobs. Each of these requires a certain degree of ritualization in order to move the individual, again, from one state to another surrounded by a sympathetic and supportive group. Examples of these institutional ritualizations include office parties for the newly promoted person, "going-away" parties for the transferred family, and other informal and formal gatherings for celebration.

As indicated in reference to group ceremonial life, our complex culture pattern in the United States and in other urban-industrial societies necessitates a mosaic of overlapping ritual communities for the enactment of multiple world views. At the private and personal level associated with family, kin, and the religious congregational community, an individual in transition is ceremonially encapsulated in sacred symbolism. At the same time, other less personal groups may be enacting ritual beliefs based on the world views of business (the office party) or science (the medical checkup). A young mother who brings her new infant for baptism and for God's blessings may on the following day take it to the pediatrician for a checkup and may herself attend a baby-care class at the Red Cross. Both belief systems—religious and scientific—are a part of her complex urban world.

I have attempted to illustrate in Figure 2 (pages 104-5) the unfolding of this life cycle within the worlds of family and kin, church or sacred meanings, and the "outside" or formal institutional world associated with science, business, and urban bureaucracy. Overlapping cultural and social worlds are the hallmark of contemporary life and must be dealt with by analysts of religion, education, and society.

Rituals for the Double World

The literature on secularization has led many churches to doubt the validity of continuing the separate sacred universe. God is supposed to have "died" or at least "entered the realm of the secular" to fuse the two realms of public and private together. This view may be theologically sound and may in essence be laudable. However, the student of human culture and of human behavior through time cannot fail to note the persistency and tenacity of our species' life. We are, after all, a part of the natural world in which rhythms and cycles are enmeshed in life itself. Human groups add symbolic interpretations to their lives, creating separate worlds for each separate culture. Ritual and symbols encode the natural raw data, giving meaning, and in the last analysis cannot be separated from our species' life. They form the heart of culture. Therefore, to effect any lasting and meaningful change within congregational communities, the educator and the change agent must take them seriously. When seen in this light the phrase "meaningless ritual" is a meaningless phrase. To appreciate the multiplicity of rituals and ceremonies is to begin to grasp the tremendous diversity and complexity of human community life.

John Comments

Gwen's essay on ceremonials was truly liberating for me; it brought a whole new world to light. For a long time Protestant church educators have neglected worship in the church. Or, at best, we've complained that the old ways no longer work and thus have wildly experimented with every new device suggested for modernizing the Sunday service.

What Gwen has done is remind us of the centrality of our total cultic life. Rites and rituals cannot be ignored, neglected, or mindlessly experimented with. Ceremonials are fundamental to our lives. They support and transmit our world view and values. Worship may not be the whole life of the church, but it is its innermost core. Where worship occurs, there is the church. It might be well for us to recall that the word orthodoxy means right worship or praise, not right opinion. What sometimes appears as useless activity may prove to be the most useful activity the church performs. In any case, Gwen's essay has made it very clear that we cannot neglect a people's rites and rituals and claim a concern for religious socialization or education.

About the same time that I was reading her essay, I came across a new book by Raymond Panikkar, *Worship and Secular Man.*[9] I studied with Dr. Panikkar at Harvard's Center for World Religions; he has an anthropological bias which always made his thoughts particularly interesting to me. As a Roman Catholic theologian whose specialty is comparative religion, he has written what I believe is a very important, insightful book on worship. Let me just mention a few of his thoughts.

He defines worship as an expression of belief or, more precisely, as a symbolic human action which arises from a particular belief. If our beliefs are intellectual, he points out, they take on intellectual forms in activities of worship such as concentration, meditation, and the like. On the other hand, if our beliefs are of the affections or heart, they express themselves in acts such as devotion, self-surrender, and praise. However, if our most worthy beliefs are related to actions performed for the sake of community, then worship will express itself in service, work, social action, and so forth.

Figure 2
LIFE CYCLE AND CEREMONIAL EVENTS

Private, Personal World

Life Crisis Transition	Ceremonial Events	Social Support Group
Birth	Prayers in church for mother and infant Minister visits Baptismal ceremony	Grandmother comes to "help with the baby" Relatives phone, send cards and gifts, attend baptism
Puberty	Communicants' class Joining the church Taking communion with congregation	Parents and kin attend service, may give a Bible or other ceremonial gift
Marriage	Counseling of couple by pastor Marriage rehearsal at church Ceremony in the church Reception at the church fellowship hall	Bride's family pays for the wedding; mother plans Friends and kinsmen of both families attend Kin send gifts, may participate in wedding party
Parenthood	Parents present child in the baptism service	Wife's mother visits and helps with household Relatives send cards and gifts
Illness	Minister visits the sick Church prays for the sick	Family helps with duties Kin gather to visit and give encouragement
Death	Prayers and visits to the survivors Church funeral Burial with minister	Kin gather for service, communal meal, sharing of consolation and help, discussion of future plans

Figure 2
LIFE CYCLE AND CEREMONIAL EVENTS

Outside, Institutional World

Institutional Transition	Expected Ritual	Social Support Group
Birth of individual into the social order	Visits to doctor and clinic Prenatal classes Assemble layette for baby Deliver infant in hospital Rest and special care at home Read "Dr. Spock"	Friends give shower, offer aid Make new friends at parents' class Doctor and nurse assist with problems Friends send letters, cards, gifts
Grades in school	Fads Dance styles, dress	Teenage cliques Sororities and fraternities
Graduation	Graduation parties and gifts	Family and kin attend and congratulate
College	Study, good grades Professionalization	Encouragement
Engagement	Announce engagement Get or give ring	Friends give parties and showers
Marriage	Plan wedding, prepare for housekeeping	Bridal showers, wedding gifts Friends are chosen for wedding party
Parenthood	See rituals for "birth"	Advice from all
Job promotion and moves	Status changes office change increasingly better house	"Going away" parties
Retirement	Say good-byes	Testimonial dinner
Hospitalization	Doctor is summoned Enter hospital Take medicine	Friends send cards or flowers
Death	Coroner issues certificate Undertaker prepares body for burial Cemetery plot chosen and arrangements made	Entire friendship and business network attends funeral, sends flowers, makes donations to charities

Likewise, if our beliefs are considered to have an essential collective expression, then worship will be considered as the work of the whole community. On the other hand, if beliefs are held to be the intimate experiences of one person, then worship will take the form of a private act. We cannot separate faith from cultic life. Too often we have forgotten that truth.

The church, from my perspective, is a community of vision and witness. Its vision is expressed in the metaphor of God's reign, a world in which peace, wholeness, harmony, justice, liberation, and community exist. That vision should be the central motif of the church's rites and rituals. As a witnessing community, the church is called to be a historical agency through which God is remaking the world and establishing his kingdom. She must therefore reorder her life and her ceremonials in such a way that she keeps that vision in focus and is an effective agent of God's historical activity. Maybe it is because we have lost sight of that faith that our rites and rituals have lost much of their meaning. Or perhaps Gwen is right when she suggests that all our rites and rituals have not lost meaning, at least not for most church members. The ceremonials which many churches engage in may actually express the faith of most churchgoers. In that case, I'd say we have lost contact with our heritage and ought to consider again Amos' prophetic protest against false cultic life: "I hate, I despise your feasts, and I take no delight in your solemn assemblies (Amos 5:21)."

But no matter; our ceremonial life is an essential aspect of religious socialization. It cannot be ignored or neglected by those concerned with the church's educational ministry. We need to explore afresh our faith and our cultic life. Perhaps then we will be ready both to renew some of our old ways and to evolve new ways to express our faith in meaningful rites and rituals.[10]

The Individual and the Life Cycle in the Educational Process

While the nature of group life is a crucial topic for understanding educational dynamics, it is of course always the individual who is taking part, learning from peers and parents, and developing values and attitudes about the universe. The child is born into a culture and cannot be fully human without it. In learning a language, communication behavior, and belief system, the child begins to classify and assign meanings to an otherwise random natural world. To understand the process through which these classifications take place is to understand learning and to begin to be able to design learning systems that will be effective.

Throughout the life cycle, education is happening. Birth, childhood, puberty, marriage, childbearing, work, menopause, retirement, and death are all learning experiences. What is communicated, and in what ways, is therefore the focus of Section Two.

Chapter 6

The Faith of Children

John H. Westerhoff III

I've always been fascinated by religious education in traditional Amish society.[1] As you may know, religion is considered so central to the Amish way of life that the Amish are opposed to religion being taught as a separate subject. Christian faith is to pervade all of life; therefore, it must be an integral part of all life and learning. For the Amish, Christianity is to be lived, not taught. Thus they are even critical of persons who rely on memorizing or quoting biblical passages. The Amish "way of life" is the proper means for communicating the word of God. Bible verses may be learned, but such learning is to be more like learning to sing hymns, speak German, or read the Bible, a part of the daily cultic life of the people. "Religious education" represents natural shared experience of community life and action. Typically, the Amish affirm that Christianity is better taught by example than by lecture. "You can teach the Bible," an Amishman is apt to say, "but if the scriptures' principles of love, forebearing, humility, and self-denial aren't practiced by those who are important to a child, I don't see where any Bible teaching will have much effect."

I find this Amish understanding of religious education insightful in a day when an increasing number of church persons are concerned that the church do a better job of teaching children the contents of the Bible and Christian beliefs. Such newly expressed desires, however noble, raise a great number of questions, not the least of which is: How do children acquire their beliefs and attitudes about God? There are still many parents who believe they need only to send their children to a church school to have them learn about God and acquire Christian faith.

Surely they do learn something in such places, but the potential learning which can occur in church schools may be both much less than and different from what we imagine. If we are truly concerned about our children's beliefs and attitudes, other factors may be more important to consider than classroom teaching.

For example: What role do familial and cultural experience have in influencing the religious beliefs and attitudes of children? That question was addressed by Ann Trevelyan, a doctoral candidate and teaching fellow at the Harvard Graduate School of Education.[2] To do so she studied four five-year-old girls from diverse cultures. Ms. Trevelyan gathered her data at different times and under different circumstances. In each case, however, she became familiar with the family by a process of participant observation; then, through organized doll play and preplanned conversations with the children, she sought to establish the relationship between their familial and cultural experience and their religious beliefs and attitudes. While her project report is not a fully documented analytical piece of research (she never made such a claim), it provides useful insight for discussion. And, more importantly, her study is helpful in understanding religious socialization. For these reasons, I'd like to share some of her findings by introducing the four children in her study.

Delores

Our first child is Delores. Delores is from the island of Jamaica. She lives in a small village a few miles above Montego Bay. Her father and mother farm a small parcel of land. They live in a small two-room cabin with an outhouse. Delores has two brothers (age six and eight) and one sister (age one). On the adjoining property live her maternal grandmother, aunt, uncle, and their children. The land owner charges them for the use of the land. By selling their produce of native Jamaican fruit and vegetables in the village market, they are able to pay their rent and some months make a small profit. While economically poor, they live close to the soil, have the necessities of life, and appear grateful for the natural world upon which they depend for their existence.

Delores most often feels that she has little control over her life or destiny. She receives little pleasure from playing with any doll given the name Delores. Good things always happen to other dolls. Her personal sense of agency and self-esteem are low. On the other hand, her ability to live in cooperative, harmonious relationships with her peers is high. When she draws herself with other children, there is always a large group of like-sized, clearly drawn male and female children. When she is with her peers she is content and happy. She has relatively low expectations that they will serve her needs or that she should serve theirs. But together they can do things—they can support each other.

Delores' parents express care for her and her siblings. They demonstrate warm feelings and love when they are together as a family, but hard work occupies most of their time. The children are the pride of their parents' lives. (They are God's gift.) But while the parents spend very little time with them, the children have each other. Rules concerning nonaggression, cooperation, and harmony are strict in Delores' family. The children must obey their parents and cause no "trouble." Delores spends much time with her kin, and she feels part of a large, happy, extended family.

The major event in the life of Delores' family (it even serves as their recreation) is attendance at a small Methodist church in the village. Attending church is a delightful, joyous occasion for Delores. At church she feels she is with those who love her. For Delores, going to church is like attending a celebration. There is no Sunday school, but all "her people" (adults and children) attend a weekly service in which they are very much physically involved. The people dance, sing, and sometimes fall into a trance. Delores looks forward to Sunday and the hike of family, friends, and neighbors to the village church.

Delores' beliefs about God correspond to her experience. God has no agency—he does not cause anything to happen in her life nor can he help her concretely. Yet God cares for her; he loves her and all children, and he has given her the warm sunshine, the sea, fish and fruit to eat, and all the beauty in nature. God has created the world for her to enjoy. She is thankful for her way of life and enjoys it. Life as she knows it is as it was meant to be, and if she appreciates life, God will always be with her. This God lacks personality or distinctive character; he is most often characterized in terms of nature or beauty. God wants her to accept and celebrate her life, to work hard and take care of the natural world. If she does so, she will know meaning and happiness.

Karen

Our second child is Karen. Karen lives in England in one of Liverpool's dockland slums. Her father is an alcoholic who works on occasion at the docks. Her mother is unemployed and expects another baby soon. She has one sister (age four) and four brothers (age six, three, two, and one). They live with her maternal grandmother in a four-bedroom government-subsidized row house with an outside toilet. Karen's father spends most of his time at the local pub. He sleeps in the morning and, if he works, does so in the afternoon. The children are made to respect their father's sleep, though he most often wakes them up upon his intoxicated return late each night.

Karen lives on the assumption that life is entirely random and cannot be depended upon. She expects little of others and demonstrates low self-esteem. When she plays with a doll named Karen, the doll is always having undesirable things happen to her. When she has her choice of a doll, she usually wants to be the mother doll. As such, she assumes domineering authority, ordering all the other dolls to do things. When Karen draws herself, she is usually in a group of other children about her size. Her relationships with her peers are at best neutral relationships of circumstance. Expecting to neither give nor receive, she doesn't make demands on them or expect they will make demands on her.

Karen's mother has numerous ambitions for Karen. She wants Karen to be "better than she is"—that is, to rise above her condition in life. She does not let Karen be dependent for a moment. Karen was weaned and toilet trained at a young age, and expected to assume responsibility from the earliest years. Correspondingly, Karen feels that she is very important to the family and lives for the praise she receives for a job well done. Her relationship with her mother is one of comradeship. She has little contact with her father. Her grandmother is a disillusioned, angry old woman who treats Karen as just one more bother, one more mouth to be fed. Karen therefore ignores her grandmother as much as possible.

Karen views adult men as worthless and mothers as put-upon

persons with too much to do. Life for Karen is hard work. She helps to take care of all the younger children and so has little time for play or peers. She feels she has little control over life and there is little to enjoy in this world.

Her family are Roman Catholics, as are all her friends and neighbors. She talks about the church as a family and the priest as her father (and father of "her family"). The priest, as a father figure, is primarily thought of as an authority figure to be believed and obeyed. Yet she loves going to church. It is the most positive aspect of her life. Most of all she loves the incense, ceremonies, music, drama of the mass, and the beauty of the church. The festivals are most enjoyable, and she participates with delight in the parades and festivities. Church is the place where you are transported into another world, a better magical world where life is joyful, fun, and rewarding.

Karen's discussion of God always switches to Jesus. (But neither Jesus nor God are thought of as male. They appear to be neuter.) God is only meaningful as Jesus, who loves children and is concerned especially for all the poor and oppressed. But Jesus is in heaven. You can be with Jesus in prayer and you can call upon him-her and he-she will help you to bear life until that wonderful, joyful day when you can be with him-her in heaven with all its beauty and reward for the poor and needy. God (Jesus) will reward her someday for working hard and being good, for believing and obeying her priest, and for going to mass.

Jane

Our third child in this study is Jane, who lives in a middle-class home in a suburb of Atlanta, Georgia. Her father is an upper-level corporate accountant; her mother a substitute school teacher. Both are college graduates. They live in a single family three-bedroom home (which they own) on a half-acre of land. They are typical white middle-class, upwardly mobile, ambitious Americans —like most everyone else in their community. She has one brother (age seven). Her grandparents live quite a distance from them, so she only sees them on special occasions.

To the adult observer, Jane seems to be extremely confident, at least when she is alone with an adult. Her sense of self-esteem and agency seem high. In doll play she wants to be a mother with a girl named Jane. As a doll, Jane demonstrates a great deal of self-confidence and is always happy, especially when she is doing what she wants by herself. But Jane does not relate well or easily to other children her own age. With them she is highly competitive and noncooperative. When she draws a group of children, she is always small and smudgy compared to the others. Jane doesn't feel at home with her peers. She expects a great deal from them, and they never come through. When she plays with dolls there is never more than one other and they often fight. She relates better to adults and feels more confident of herself and at home in an adult world.

She has a dependent relationship with her mother, expecting to follow instructions so she can learn to grow up to be like her mother. Her parents will take care of her. All she needs to do is accept their control. Happiness results. She highly respects her father and wants to marry someone just like him. He is the final authority in her life, and pleasing him is her greatest joy.

Her parents give her and her brother a great deal of attention. But she and her brother are very competitive at home; they are not friends. As a result she tends to be highly individualistic, with a tremendous ambition to succeed.

Jane's family belongs to a Methodist church. Church is utterly dull, boring, and meaningless to her. She attends a Sunday church school but derives little pleasure from it. Her parents are very much involved in the life of the church, so she goes to please them. She does not view the church as a community, only as a place to be endured because it pleases her parents. As a result she acts as if she enjoys church but in play reveals mostly negative feelings. Church is a place to be quiet, to be told things you do not understand, and be with people you don't want to be with. The minister's only identity is as someone who talks a lot to adults.

For Jane, God is just like her father—strong, serious, hardworking, concerned primarily for his own—that is, people like her family and those who go to Jane's church. She has no idea of God being concerned about others (the poor, for example). Yet God can do anything he wants. For Jane, God is definitely a white male who takes care of her, but she must be good and obedient in return. God doesn't bring much joy, but it's important to do as he wants so he will love you and give you what you want.

Brenda

Our last child is Brenda, who lives in a three-room low-income high-rise apartment in Chicago, Illinois. It is in an all-black neighborhood. She lives with her grandmother, mother, two sisters (age seven and eight), and one brother (age three). The whereabouts of Brenda's father is not known, though he returns for a week to a month from time to time. Her mother and grandmother are both domestic servants for white families living in Chicago's suburbs.

Brenda receives little pleasure from playing with a doll named Brenda. She demonstrates little self-esteem or feelings of personal worth. However, she does relate well with her peers. She is most at home with the give and take of peer group play. She feels good about herself when she is in a group. She cooperates well, showing low levels of aggression and competition.

Brenda sees her mother only in the evening; hence Brenda is expected (even at five) to take care of herself, although she knows she can call on an aunt who lives in the next apartment house if she needs help. In the evening her mother is tired and has little time for her. Yet she feels loved, but something of a nuisance and perhaps unwanted. These feelings of being loved and perhaps not wanted are in tension. All she knows is that she has to make it on her own, although she has the helping hand of her older siblings who care about her and will help her. In fact, all the children support each other, spend lots of time together, and are very close. But she knows they can't help her too much for they must first of all take care of themselves. As a result, she doesn't expect much from them. She loves her father most but wishes he were home more, for when he is home he gives her a great deal of attention and she feels particularly secure and loved.

Her family is active in an all-black Baptist church. She loves church, especially the singing. She feels a part of a special community. All the adults and children are very close. The preacher's sermons about "hell and damnation" confuse her, but the "emotional" nature of the service is very important in her life. She describes a close bond with "her people" and sees the church as a place where people "care" and have fun. There's joy and hope at church. The preacher tells her how she should live, helps her to feel close to God.

For Brenda, God is central in her life—he is Jesus who loves her like her father but also is very stern and demanding like her mother. God really cares for people like herself, even though he makes demands upon them. God isn't able to do much for her now (in this world), but someday he will help her if she lives the sort of life the preacher says. At the same time God is concerned about her all the time, though not always near her. Her future reward in seeking forgiveness for "bad actions" and being good is his approval and the joy of knowing he likes her even though no one else may. And most of all that he will see to it that someday she has everything she wants in heaven. She therefore accepts life as it is now and lives for that future.

An Analysis and Implications

All these descriptions are incomplete, but if nothing else they demonstrate the significant role which family, culture, and church experience play in the acquisition and formation of a child's religious beliefs and attitudes. Children are socialized into their beliefs and attitudes about God. It seems as if children cannot have understandings of God which are distinctly different from their experience, or, to put it another way, children's understandings of God are directly dependent upon their experiences.

Now there is nothing revolutionary in that conclusion; it's just that we seem continually to forget it, or perhaps more importantly we neglect to make use of that insight when we plan religious education. And it's that concern to which I'd like to turn now.

Clarifying Our Educational Mission

To begin, let us reflect on a Christian world view and value system. Religious education is a dependent discipline. Unless we are clear on our understanding and way of life, we cannot engage mindfully in religious education. A world view corresponds to our understanding of life, a value system to our way of life. Together they provide religious education with its goals. (The words "educational mission" when applied to Christian education refer to those goals; the words "educational ministry" refer to our methods.) If it is a Christian world view and value system we intend to communicate, obviously a central task is to identify exactly what constitutes such an understanding and way of life.

Too often we have thrown our energies into educational programs in the church with no clear idea of where we intend to go or why. I've seen churches get excited about the latest educational technique, such as individualized programmed instruction, and immediately try to program the learning of biblical content without even asking for what end. Others have gotten so enamored of a desire for community that they have proceeded to act as if a sense of community is a valid end, in and by itself, only rarely asking if meaningful religious community needs to be related to some goal beyond itself. Still other people have gotten their eyes so glued to some laudable aim, such as liberation, that they were unaware that they were using oppressive means to reach it. Obviously it's impossible to achieve such a way of life unless our ends and means correspond.

Christian education is dependent upon a clear understanding of the word Christian. What does the name imply? What human behaviors, toward what historical end? Unless those questions are answered and agreed upon, a church cannot (and indeed ought not) proceed to plan its educational ministry. We just can't have a mindful educational ministry without a clear vision of our educational mission.

Every religious community will have its own definitions and shared understandings. But for me a Christian world view and value system look something like this:

There is a reality other than ourselves, our experiences, and the world. I call this reality God. We cannot understand ourselves without understanding the nature and character of God, even though we acknowledge that God may not be directly or completely accessible to us. What we do affirm is that we can know God through his/her own self-disclosures revealed in historical actions in all women and men, but particularly in Jesus, the Christ. Because of these self-disclosures, I believe that history is going somewhere—it is ordered from beyond itself by intentional, purposive activity, moving history toward a goal. That goal is expressed in the Bible by the concept of shalom and in the metaphor of the reign of God—a vision of community, peace, and justice. I believe that a transcendent agent (God) is working in, on, and through the world—including us—to actualize that goal.

This meaningful vision upon which we must base our individual and corporate lives is best understood as the realization of values such as harmony, peace, justice, wholeness, partnership, health,

cooperation, welfare, community, nonviolence, freedom, liberation, security, sanity, and a concrete concern for the outsider,
the poor, the hurt, the needy, the captive, and the oppressed.

As persons we are historical beings. That means we actualize
ourselves in history; we are made by and we make history. Men
and women have a tendency to be estranged from God's vision
and action. We distort it. We act against it. And yet it slowly and
surely comes—often, in spite of the majority of us, because a
faithful remnant, however unpure, acts. And so we are called to
unite with others and join God in his/her historical action to
realize shalom. We are called to turn our lives around and live
as if God's reign has arrived—to express in our individual and
corporate lives those beliefs, attitudes, and actions which point
to the realization of God's kingdom of community, peace, and
justice. To have that understanding of life and to live that way
of life is to be Christian.

But enough. That's at best a beginning summary of my world
view and value system, my conviction as to the church's educational mission. Obviously, that which these words symbolize
is very important to me, but I trust no one will think that I believe
transmitting or memorizing such words is equivalent to the
church's educational ministry. Neither is an understanding of our
educational goals the primary focus of this essay. Rather, this
essay is concerned with the style of life which results from a
people's understanding of life and the experiences children have
as they interact with meaningful others.

Children are my concern. Through the years I've often been
misunderstood as being unconcerned for children in the church.
What I'd like to make clear once and for all is that I am very
concerned about children. It is because I am so concerned
about them that I recommend we center our attention on adults.
Why? Well, consider first where children are initially introduced
to their understanding of life and way of life—in the home and
family, with its adult examples and advocates. Second, consider
what community of life and mission they are inducted into—the
Christian church, an adult community! No matter what we attempt
to communicate to children in the home or church, it will be
communicated by adults who cannot communicate what they
themselves do not affirm and live. The educational crisis in the
church is a crisis in the faith and actions of adults. A world view

and value system are verbal abstractions. Our style of life and behavior are concrete; it is they which children experience, and in turn it is those experiences which frame their understanding and way of life.

Whether focusing on adult life-styles implies the conversion or resocialization of adults into new understandings and ways of behavior or the continuing education of adults so that they might more fully and completely live old understandings and ways of behavior has to be decided upon in each community situation and with each person. But in either case, adults will have to be a primary concern of our ministry on behalf of children; they are the agents of all religious socialization.

Planning an Educational Ministry

Aware of my socialization bias, if I were a local church educator who had chosen to center my educational efforts on adults so they might be enabled to act out more fully the understanding and way of life I described earlier, I would choose a strategy related to life in two institutions—the family and the congregation. That strategy would include concern for experience within and action by both institutions. Here is a small glimpse of what I might attempt to do, through the planning and decision-making of those who are to be involved.

First, I would like to establish groups of parents and other concerned adults meeting in homes to discuss our Christian faith and heritage in the context of their lives and history. I hope that these communities would be consciously evaluating, reforming, and renewing their lives. They would be asking painful questions, such as: What sort of role models do we present to our children? What sort of experiences do we offer our children? What values are affirmed? What understanding of life and way of life is transmitted? How can we support each other in living the life we desire? How can we aid each other in the socialization of our children into our peculiar understanding and style of life? Small house churches, preschools or day-care centers at the church, summer communities, weekend vacation retreats, and the like might be discussed as contexts for purposeful religious socialization. Based upon such decisions, the educational program, resources, and funding could be planned and supported.

Second, I would like to use each group, committee, board, and organization in the church as contexts for engaging the leadership and members of the church in evaluating, reforming, and renewing their corporate lives as a community of faith. Here questions would be addressed which relate every experience persons have with or within the church—for example, buildings, rites and rituals, organization, leadership, and actions in the world—to the Christian faith and life. Again, our aim would be to establish the understanding of life and the way of life we wish to sustain and transmit. Thereby we would be discovering how we need to change individually and corporately so as to have our corporate life correspond to our vision of a Christian community of faith. In other words, I would hope to make the renewal and reformation of the church, its organization and structures, a primary concern of religious education. At the same time I would like to structure the educational program so that the church, in everything it did, was consciously involved in that renewing, reforming process.

Third and last, working through the same structures I have just described, I would like to engage the church in an evaluation of the social forces which prevent or enable positive socialization into Christian faith to take place in both our community and nation. Such efforts would involve a look at such very diverse phenomena as the social isolation of suburban communities, competition and oppression in the school system, the economic needs of the poor and elderly, justice in the courts, national priorities, and television programs. With a vision clearly in mind and an awareness of the need for change, the church could then engage in corporate social action. Educational program, resources, and funding could be planned so as to enable that action and reflection to take place.

Now when the church had fully engaged its adults in the renewal and reformation of their individual and corporate lives, when they had established structures to sustain and transmit their way of life and understanding of life to the world and to the next generation, then I would like to proceed to plan for specific supportive educational efforts with children, teaching-learning efforts as distinct from intentional socialization efforts. Ideally these teaching-learning efforts in the church would be occurring simultaneously with intentional socialization in the home and church. That's what I'd really like. But I'm not sure it's possible, and I fear that the crucial effort of reformation and renewal of adults and their communities will get lost if we do not make them a priority. Further, I have a suspicion that the program I have projected for working with adults will occupy the major portion of our available time. Therefore, while teaching-learning programs specifically for children are to be affirmed and recommended, I suggest we begin working with adults so as to make sure that our processes of socialization at home and in the church intentionally correspond to our understanding of Christian faith and life.

To summarize: The faith of our children is directly related to their experiences at home and in the church. A community of faith, therefore, needs to be clear about its educational mission, its understanding and way of life. The church further needs to deliberately engage in an educational ministry which reflects its mission in its corporate life and action. To do that is to focus our attention on intentional socialization of adults and children at home and in the church. That isn't far from what the Amish seem to do naturally.

Now while the religious beliefs and attitudes of children are a major concern of many parents and educators, an even more verbalized concern focuses upon values. My position on the transmission of values is similar to my stand on the transmission of beliefs and attitudes. The learning of values could easily have been integrated into this essay. However, since that issue is one of such pressing importance, I've chosen to deal with it separately. Nevertheless, it would be helpful if the two chapters were understood as having a single point of view—namely, that structure and experience are essential aspects of socialization.

Chapter 7

The Learning of Values

John H. Westerhoff III

Few issues are of greater concern to parents and educators than values. In a multitude of ways, they ask: How can we teach children our values? A mass of printed matter has appeared which attempts to give an answer. Whether or not we can deliberately teach children values remains unresolved, though opinions abound. Almost two decades ago Louis Raths, Merrill Harmin, and Sidney Simon wrote a book entitled *Values and Teaching*.[1] They took a position on that issue. And today their thoughts have become a movement, a movement founded upon a technique known as "values clarification."[2]

Values clarification began as a concern for the emotional health of children and the inability of many children to learn as well as they might because they lacked a clear set of values. Aware of the confusing set of diverse values presented to children and bounded by the limited role schools can play, these educators evolved an imaginative solution to this problem.

Defining a value as something chosen freely, from alternatives, after thoughtful consideration of the consequences, something a person cherishes and is willing to affirm publicly, and something acted upon consistently, they devised a technique for aiding persons to clarify their values. It caught on. Throughout the country enthusiastic supporters of values clarification preached and practiced its methods in churches and schools. I've been among them; in fact, I still count myself an advocate. Yet in recent days I've begun to question a hidden assumption. To concentrate on the process of values clarification is to imply that there is no way persons can sustain and transmit to the next generation particular values.

While still convinced it is helpful to assist persons in the clarification of their values, I've become more concerned with where values come from in the first place. It's just too simple (and erroneous) to say they are acquired by values clarification. More convincing is the argument that values are learned in numerous and diverse unconscious ways, ways directly related to how persons learn their culture. Educational techniques such as values clarification are useful in showing how values can be understood and reinforced through values clarification, but there are more basic issues to be addressed. At least, that is the assumption and rationale behind my continuing quest for new insights into "the learning of values."

A Study of Values

In that search, I discovered *People of Rimrock,*[3] a comparative study of values in five cultures conducted by a group of Harvard anthropologists in the Rimrock area of western New Mexico. Here communities of Navaho and Zuñi Indians, Spanish Americans, Mormons, and Texan homesteaders live side by side, providing investigators with five contrasting cultures in a single area. The Rimrock comparative study of values and their cultural transmission has significantly influenced my present thinking.

First of all, it has caused me to reconsider the radical role which the family plays in the acquisition of values, especially during the childhood years. And secondly, it has encouraged me to focus my attention on the structure of the family and the nature of its child-rearing practices as two significant factors in the transmission of values. But to begin, let me in a very summary fashion describe the results of the Rimrock field research on the families of the Texas homesteaders and the Zuñi Indians.

The Zuñi Child

The world of the Zuñi child consists of a large extended family (the child's own parents and siblings along with his or her matrilineally related aunts, uncles, and grandparents) living in a single medium-sized dwelling. Authority rests jointly with the child's grandmother and her brother, who, while living somewhere nearby, is considered an "associate member" of the family. A Zuñi father works in community economic enterprises (mostly sheep raising) which unite the men from numerous households in shared leadership and responsibility.

The Zuñi infant receives the constant attention of a wide variety of persons for the first three years of life. Fed on a demand schedule, the Zuñi child is weaned and toilet trained at a late age (two to three years). Little is expected of the child during these early years. At about three, this indulgence is brought to an abrupt end. But even then, the child is not urged or expected to assume any family responsibilities. The Zuñi child is simply encouraged to be with adults and thus observe their behavior. Nevertheless, from birth on, one particular way of life is a dominant concern of child-rearing. A Zuñi child must learn to always keep his or her temper and never fight. Through constant reasoning (never force or punishment), a child is helped to acquire a nonaggressive understanding of life.

For them, early childhood is the time for play. In the extended Zuñi household there are typically a cousin or two of every child's own age to play with, as well as numerous other siblings who act as role models and caretakers. The Zuñi child, never alone, is always a conscious member of a caring community which emphasizes cooperative, harmonious living.

Texas Homesteaders

The Texas homesteaders, on the other hand, reveal entirely different family structures and child-rearing practices. The typical Texan child is born into a small nuclear family consisting of a father, mother, and one or two siblings. The father is self-employed; he works his own land, sharing his profits only with his wife and children. The mother is home alone most of the day to do the housework and care for the children. However, since homesteader mothers assume many outside responsibilities, such as the family garden, the young child is often left in the house alone. This nuclear household cannot approach the personal attention available for infant care among the Zuñis. These homesteader mothers, therefore, tend to feed their infants on strict schedules, just as they wean and toilet train them as early as possible. Of necessity, the young child learns to be alone at a young age.

During childhood, the homesteader child has few playmates, rarely any his or her own age. Siblings are often at school or uninterested in playing with younger children. Since these Texan families most often live at great distance from neighbors, the children lack playmates. As a result they are left most of the time to their own devices.

Another striking difference between the Zuñi and Texan families is aggression. The homesteader family most often permits quarreling and fighting among young children and their playmates so they will learn to settle arguments for themselves. And when parents do correct what they believe is negative behavior (quarreling or fighting that has gone "too far"), they most often use some form of mild physical punishment. Homesteader children are urged to do tasks by themselves and are praised when they succeed. They are given responsibility as soon as they can understand the word. The homesteader child is most often alone and encouraged to take care of himself or herself—that is, to be independent and responsible as soon as possible.

Effects of Child-rearing

Obviously this is a superficial summary of the Rimrock research. Of greatest interest, however, are the apparent effects of these two very differently structured families and their child-rearing practices. What becomes most obvious is the major role early socialization plays in the acquisition of values.

In testing the children from these two sets of families, the researchers at Rimrock discovered significant differences in values. The homesteader children, for example, were overwhelmingly concerned with success and achievement. The Texan child was apt to say, "I want to be a rancher and raise cattle so I can get money" or "I want to be a great Yankee baseball player; I'll be the pitcher." In contrast, the most popular Zuñi ambition is to be a man or a woman without specific qualifications, or more simply to be a Zuñi. Consistently it was discovered that the homesteader children lived by the values of competition and aggression, while the Zuñi children exemplified cooperation and nonaggression.

The hypothesis of the Rimrock study suggests that the structure of the family played a major role in determining which values are most beneficial, thereby influencing which values are affirmed and transmitted. For example, the Zuñis' large extended family and their crowded living conditions necessitated a concern for the values of harmony, cooperation, and a strict control of aggression.

The Evolving of Values

The study further states that the ancestors of the Zuñis did not live in an extended family pueblo or have the same values as today. It was after the modern Zuñis' family structures evolved that they discovered aggression needed to be controlled. It is the Rimrock study's thesis that this adaptation occurred very rapidly and that significant changes in child-rearing resulted. They admit that the value system of the "pre-family-crisis Zuñis" is lost in the past, but they presume that the emphasis of the modern Zuñis on the values of harmony, cooperation, and non-aggression are directly related to the development of the extended family which necessitated a severe control of aggression and competition.

It is easier to investigate this hypothesis by studying Anglo cultures, for they have lengthier written traditions. The forebears of the Texas panhandlers, for example, came from a common culture in the British Isles. Their immigration to America resulted in a dramatic change in family structure. It was a change similar to that which is believed to have occurred in Zuñi society, but in reverse. British culture prior to their immigration was characterized by an extended patriarchal family living in a single household. As long as this "Elizabethan" family was the cultural ideal, children were weaned relatively late, fed on self-demand schedules, and given a great deal of attention. Within the home, dependence was more valued than independence, and obedience more valued than freedom. Children were believed to be born evil and potentially aggressive; it was the duty of parents to control such tendencies by stern discipline.

The Elizabethan family fell upon hard times soon after the arrival in America of the colonists. The family head did not know how to cope with new and strange environment any better than their children. Furthermore, patriarchs often engaged in the menial labor of necessary survival, with the result that their authority was sharply challenged.[4]

Not only was patriarchal authority challenged, but, with the availability of frontier land, the extended family gave way to a nuclear type, well suited to westward movement. The isolation of the family unit necessitated independent and competitive lifestyles. Independence supplanted obedience as a goal of socialization. Coincident with these changes in socialization goals were changes in child-rearing aims and practices. Child-rearing changed to meet the demands of a new family structure. New values were needed and new values emerged. The Texan family relaxed the formerly extended family's pressure on the control of aggression and the requirement of obedience, substituting an exaggerated early demand for independence. Whereas British parents in preimmigration times may have feared that their children would be aggressive and disobedient, a major concern of these Texan parents was that their children might be excessively dependent.

As the ancestors of the Texans (and Zuñis) underwent a social crisis, change in their family structure resulted. In turn, their values and child-rearing practices were altered. Each of these cultures was characterized by a period of stability in family structure, values, and socialization patterns which was interrupted by a period of rapid change and followed by another period of stability. Today the Zuñis need not protect themselves against predatory neighbors, yet they continue to live in extended family households, react negatively to all forms of aggression, and insist on harmony and cooperation as important values. The Texans no longer rely upon individual conquest of the untamed frontier, yet they continue to live in small nuclear families which affirm the value of competition, aggression, and individualism.

Implications for Religious Education

The conclusion of the Rimrock study is that certain historical crises may require a society to modify its social structures, particularly its family organization. These changes in turn may require changes in values. As the values change to meet the needs of society, so will socialization practices. And thus a new process of socialization will transmit to the next generation the family's newly affirmed values.

Most enlightening to me is the suggestion of a direct interrelationship between historical social conditions, the structure of the family, cultural values, and socialization, and, correspondingly, the importance of a hidden curriculum in family life, structure, and child-rearing practices for the affirmation and acquisition of values. It is interesting to note that today, in the face of a number of social crises in American culture, we see increasingly a new generation experimenting with a variety of different family structures. Correspondingly, those who move into communes typically affirm dominant values of cooperation over competition, harmony over aggression, group consciousness over individual consciousness, and so on. We also notice changes in child-rearing practices within these same changing families.

Increasingly, there are some of us who believe that we face a historical crisis. The old way of life and its values are no longer adequate. We talk about those emerging values which need to replace our culture's traditional values, but we have difficulty overcoming the estrangement between our ideal and manifest values. We have difficulty transmitting and sustaining the new values we intellectually affirm. We want one set of values, but we live according to another, often uneasily. Those of us who affirm an interest in religious socialization need to confront this agonizing issue head on.

Some of us have concluded that the small nuclear family, living in relative isolation from others, is doomed to engage in child-rearing practices which will tend to transmit values and a way of life we can no longer affirm, a way of life and values no longer satisfactory for our times. We are aware that we need to look seriously at our families, their structures and child-rearing practices. This is a painful process. We have been socialized to believe our present family structures and values are "God-given" or, at least, the way things ought to be. Our social crisis is not yet all-encompassing enough to force radical change. For such reasons I'm not sure how many of us will ever be able, on our own, to make any major changes in family structure or child-rearing. Even though we may desire a wider family group, most of us do not live anywhere near our kin and still suffer from a high level of mobility. Since we are just not up to communal family living, it appears that the small nuclear family with parents and a couple of children living in a number of single family dwellings and separated from kin will be our lot for some time to come.

The Church as a New Family

Is there nothing, then, we can do about our concern for the acquisition and transmission of new values for ourselves and our children? The church could provide us with an answer.

A small, closely knit church could become a model for an extended family. A small church community reading the signs of the time in the same way, committed to the same values, and willing to give major attention to community life could so structure itself and live that new values might be evolved, sustained, and transmitted. I have just begun to imagine a few things such churches would need to concentrate upon. These include such actions as providing preschools and day-care facilities for all children—that is, facilities where men and women would both on occasion share intimate life with other adults and groups of children. Further, such church communities would need to unite, as often as possible, at least three generations for activities together. Small house churches might evolve as subunits of a much larger community, but each should include both sexes, married and unmarried, older and younger, with and without children. Self-conscious multigenerational groupings would need to spend a significant amount of time together for diverse activities but could join with others for important rituals and ceremonials. They could also build and actively participate in summer communities or weekend and vacation gatherings.

My point is this: If a congregation takes seriously the importance of family structure and early child-rearing practices, it could evolve a structure and process for intentional socialization through which the values which are consistent with the Christian faith and most demanded by the world in which we are moving could be evolved, sustained, and transmitted. Obviously, such radical changes in local churches would not be easily realized. A corresponding change in family life would also be necessary and equally as difficult. There's a host of problems in this proposal. One can question whether the church can ever become this sort of community. Or are there enough families in one place willing to put this much energy and investment into a new sort of extended family-faith community?

This essay does not confront these problems and questions head on, just as it does not frame a clear picture of such faith communities. What it does suggest is that those who are concerned about religious socialization discuss these issues. Those of us who are truly concerned for the biblical doctrine of shalom (and the metaphor of the kingdom of God), need to explore the values that are inherent in those images, values such as harmony, cooperation, wholeness, nonaggression, unity, corporateness, peace, justice, and concern for the outsider and the oppressed. And if we conclude that such values are worth living for and worth passing on to the next generation, then we must surely consider the structure of our families and their child-rearing practices. The time seems right for such conversations. What we know about values and socialization should help us to be more mindful. It will not be as easy or as much fun as values clarification, but it may enable us to join God in his action to establish the reign of shalom in history. Surely values, the family, and child-rearing practices are fundamental to that mission.

Gwen Comments

In John's two essays on children and on values he has put forth an important hypothesis based on other studies and other data which share his starting point. I happen to be one of those who shares such a position, and it is essentially this: that structure communicates content. Put in another way, the *medium* of the family form, with its highly predictable prescribed behaviors, communicates the *message* that the child receives regarding what things and behaviors are to be valued and pursued.

As a child in church I often heard the preacher say as a sermon illustration that "what you *do* speaks so loudly that I cannot hear what you *say*." My mother was fond of repeating the old adage, "Actions speak louder than words," and also the admonition "Beauty is more than skin deep" or "Pretty is as pretty does." All these give intellectual assent to the idea that people learn from behavioral interaction and from observation, not from words. At the same time, they are judged not by their words or looks but by their behaviors.

The idea of family structure as the basic communicator of values has been explored in depth by a number of anthropologists interested in culture and personality.[5] There seems to be a recurring congruence in every culture—complex as well as simple—between the structures and processes of family and community life and the learning of values. Dorothy Lee calls the process of learning a world view "the codification of reality." It includes the way in which a child *encodes* the universe, what meanings are placed on inanimate objects such as rocks and trees, and how simple biological needs such as food-getting, elimination, and sex are transformed into symbolic events imbued with deeper significance.

One of the most basic biological realities that human cultures must deal with and transform into symbolic meanings is the reality of sex. In primitive society we see a wide variety of symbolic meanings arising around what women do, who they are in the meaning system, and in which activities they cannot be allowed to participate. Men are also defined in every world view, and their place is taught to little boys by precept and example. In many preliterate cultures the women are tied inextricably into their biological function as childbearers and as food-getters. Yet these are two functions that are indispensable for a culture to survive and transmit its lore to the next generation.

In our own society we have given lip service in the churches and in the public schools to the freedom and the equality of all individuals. Yet the *structure* of our society and preferred family form is one in which one sex is relegated to childbearing and child-rearing and the other to active competition for scarce resources—namely, money.

With such a dichotomy of labor activities, a set of meanings and values must accompany and justify what we are in fact doing in order to preserve our way of life. The values are tied to a dual universe of flesh (women) and spirit (men) and to the necessity and importance of the mother in a biologically bound everpresent union with the child. This may be elaborated into other values: "Women are better with children than men," "Women are naturally loving and nurturing people," "Women are good with details but not good with thinking abstract thoughts," "Women are good in home economics, or typing, or beauty school but not in physics, calculus, medicine, or law."

I have tried to explain some of the dynamics of keeping women in their place as a side effect of the cultural impetus to preserve and transmit the lore of a people. The women have acted as cultural transmitters in our Euro-American religions. My chapter on sex and socialization speaks of value learning but also of freedom, dignity, and human liberation.

Chapter 8

Sex and Socialization [1]

Gwen Kennedy Neville

Within the overall process of the individual's religious socialization there exists an internal process that is decidedly different for male and female persons. In approaching the formidable topic of religious socialization, I will concentrate on three central issues in the process of women's enculturation into set roles in our society.

The first is *learning,* the subtle process of acquiring all the necessary behaviors to successfully act out the role of "woman" within a particular community's way of life.

The second is *culture.* But at the outset, let me disavow any belief in the abstract construct of an overall "American culture" or even a WASP culture. White Anglo-Saxon Protestant is a label for a category of people, lumped together because they would share certain traits if they were printed out on someone's computer. Such cultural and social categories are interesting, but it is not within general labels that people learn to be male or female. They learn these meanings and behaviors within real human groups. Cultural groups are made up, in this sense, of interacting webs of real people involved in personal kin and religious relationships extending over a transgenerational time period and over a particular geographical space. I have spoken of these groups within American society as "subcultures" because they exist as internal systems within the larger systems of the metropolis and the national body politic. They are sometimes invisible, but they emerge to express commonality at special times. As socializing agents, cultural groups are formidable in their effectiveness.

And the third issue is *liberation,* a concept that has been so much bandied about that we all probably wonder if anything new remains to be said, and if we understand the tenacity of culture, we wonder if liberation is possible. If so, I hope to look at some alternative cultural arrangements that may enable and accompany liberated life-styles.

Framing the Question

In 1966, somewhere on the road to liberation, I asked a very liberated friend of mine how she had become so free. This particular friend had completed her B.D. at a fine theological seminary, served as an associate pastor in California, had taken part in the early student movement, and had married a bright young classmate who was also a pastor. She was intelligent, charming, and had a good job doing interesting things. So, interested in ascertaining how she had broken out of her traditional cultural past in Tennessee, I asked, "How did you get so free?"

Her reply was, after some thought, "I think I just read the Bible and believed it."

After six years, I crossed paths with the same woman. She was now a housewife and mother, working in volunteer groups while her husband taught on the faculty of a large state university. Both had been honor students at seminary. *He* went back for a Ph.D. while she had two babies. *He* interviewed nationally and found a good job as an assistant professor, while she patiently waited to move with him. *He* writes lectures, books, and articles, while she donates her time at the church and at the local political party headquarters and plans to get back to school "someday when the children are a little older." What happened to the freedom, to believing the Bible? It looked as if cultural programming had been effective. Tennessee won, in the last analysis.

I had seen it happen to one after another of my friends and to myself in intermittent doses. We had each one "believed it"— the Bible, the public-school party line about all individuals being equal, the national political speeches about giving the same opportunities to all. At the conscious, rational level we were all raised to believe that we should seek an education and that we could be anything we wanted to be. Many girls I knew had gone to college and on to graduate school. But somewhere along the way, by the time of the tenth high school reunion, all the boys had miraculously turned into orthodontists and veterinarians and petroleum engineers, and most of the girls had simply turned into mommies. Something had happened that I couldn't explain. Something invisible was going on that had sabotaged everyone's good intentions. The search for an explanation has continued to occupy me as I miraculously, after already becoming a mommy, have turned into an anthropologist.

Learning

With the best intentions, thousands of girls graduate from college every year and start out merrily on a job. Thousands of others finish graduate school and become physicians and lawyers. Their teachers have praised them and encouraged them to their best ability, and they have believed of themselves that they are "different" and will be able to succeed at having a career, possibly combining it with marriage and a family. Many do succeed, but under great disadvantages and with a great deal more guilt and conflict than they had ever dreamed would be necessary.

Others succumb to the demands of culture—embodied in their mothers and aunts and husbands and their inner consciences. It is so much easier to do it "their way." For even the most liberated of active professional women, after all, has a mother. And the mother, in addition to being very proud of her daughter's success, will be very worried about her grandchildren's welfare. She will almost certainly appoint herself as personal reminder to the daughter that she is lucky to have such a good husband who "lets her continue working." Even more common is the mother who continually warns the daughter that if she doesn't watch out she will "lose her husband to another woman who will treat him with more attention and indulgence and not boss him around so much."

Every woman, in addition to her mother, has aunts and grandmothers in the wings somewhere, and, if she is married, a mother-in-law, and then of course her husband's aunts and grandmothers. Then there are all the assorted fathers, stepfathers, uncles, and brothers who have assigned themselves the task of spoiling the little girl and keeping the big girl in line. In the comic strip *Dennis the Menace,* Gina is seen explaining to Joey that he has to be a proper brother to his new baby sister and "see that she marries the right guy." The process of induction into culturally approved ways begins in the bassinet.

Through the handling and treatment of little girls and little boys, the way they are dressed and the toys they are given, we know that culture is transmitted in invisible ways. Edward Hall calls this "the silent language"—the language of actions and relationships that in early years gives loud instructions to girl and boy children of how they must act out their social roles.

In looking closely at this learning process, we see several principles clearly at work in shaping sex roles and transmitting cultural expectations.

1. The first principle has to do with levels of learning. Women in our society are socialized on two levels—the verbal, rational, public level (what teachers and parents and churches *say*) and the invisible, behavioral, private level (what teachers and parents and churches *do*). At the conscious level, my friend's clergyman probably stood up for human liberation. Her mother encouraged her to make good grades in school. But meanwhile, at home, other signals were communicated to her so efficiently that at the proper moment, when triggered by certain cues, she voluntarily gave up her own career for her husband's and began the cycle of being a mother. Psychological studies have demonstrated the persistency of these learning experiences. From the point of view of the student of culture, the reason for this persistency of early learning is that it takes place within a religious-kin unit.

It is in this group that the individual finds his or her identity and receives the set of cultural instructions that enables a child to become an adult among that people. In less complex societies, of course, the kin-religious network lives near one another and operates for many activities. In an urbanized world, the kin network is often scattered and the religious-kin community establishes itself only periodically for family-centered events.

In enactment of the play, which is the way of life, culture is transmitted to the child by the people. They do so as they act in their roles of "aunt," "uncle," "friend of the family," "parish minister," and so on, by just doing what uncles and aunts do and expecting the child to do what nephews and nieces do. At the same time, in different settings the child sees the roles of public life: teacher, minister, politician. A highly important transmission of culture is taking place at both these levels.

2. Growing out of this understanding of the nature of two-level learning, a second principle could be stated as follows:

Women learn their expected roles as culture-bearers through interaction in a specific subcultural or ethnic-religious community. Each subcultural religious group will have specific roles for men and women. Each sex will have assigned tasks and activities that are required and others that are taboo. For instance, in a Protestant worship service in the American Northeast, the family group will be seated together in the same pew. In the same city at the Orthodox synagogue, mothers and daughters will sit behind a screen so that the men and boys will not see them and be distracted from the serious business of prayers. Girls growing up in both these traditions may attend public schools and be taught the same amalgamated American virtues. But their social reality is very different from one another and from that purveyed in the school textbook.

As pointed out in my earlier lengthy discussion on ritual and ceremonial life, it is within the religious services that core meanings and sacred values of each cultural group are acted out in time and space—all the values and beliefs and marriage patterns and holy observances that are necessary in order for that culture to survive as an entity. Ceremonials are a preservative of culture—and human beings cannot exist without a culture-community matrix. Inside the stereotyped events that go into preparing for Thanksgiving or Passover, a girl child learns what it means to be a woman and a man in that culture.

In a sort of mini-ritual, the same values and beliefs about women, men, and the world are acted out all over again every week on Sunday morning at 11:00 A.M. (or at sabbath services on Friday night). Sitting behind the screen at the synagogue enacts spatially the belief that women are inferior to men and that their presence too near the altar will pollute the holy paraphernalia. In Catholic masses the same spatial separation, in which women are not allowed to come to the altar or to administer the sacraments, communicates similar messages to the child. In Protestant churches this space barrier has only recently been broken down regarding the sacraments and performance of sacred functions in worship, and as recently as ten years ago the total absence of women on church boards taught the little girl effectively that the business of the church was men's business. Their mommies' business was to organize church circles and family-night suppers in a separate, special, female arena of activity.

The fact that these messages have been well learned is exemplified by the number of women today in their twenties and thirties who want very much in their heads to be liberated and to break the mold. We want to try equal living within the church or the university, but we suffer from frustration, conflict, and ulcers in the whole situation. No matter how much we desire interaction as equals, we fall into the traps of saying we will make the coffee or take the minutes of the meeting. Our beliefs about reality have been programmed into us and stamped with supernatural approval.

In addition to learning through the use of space and division of labor at these high ceremonial occasions, the little girl is learning from the *language* used by the religious community. This is a language in which all references to the deity are couched in male pronouns and in which the hymns all refer blatantly to Christian soldiers or to men of God, verbally codifying the little girl's reality into a cognitive set which classifies her *out* of any meaningful participation. She is also exposed to word and picture language in Sunday school curricula in which boys are active and assertive in doing interesting things and girls sit by and watch out of windows.[2] She is taught by a female teacher, who is a mommy, and she is preached to in the sanctuary by a male person who talks about "all mankind" and the relation of God to man. In Hebrew school, in much of Catholic education, and in many conservative Protestant groups she is taught in a group of all girls after about the fourth grade, a group which learns that they will someday marry the boys in the other group and live happily ever after.

Culture

It is obvious in having looked at these aspects of learning that they are all tied up with aspects of culture. Learning can be legitimately defined, in one sense, simply as cultural transmission.

What is transmitted, in all?

The answer is: a way of organizing reality into meaningful categories and assigning labels to things. The world view of a culture is expressed in its social arrangements and has its roots in the natural environmental niche to which it is adapted.

Now, since in the United States we are dealing with cultures that have been ripped out of their European environments and reinstated in new locations, the process of tracing becomes more important. Anderson and others have pointed out that European cultures have been translated on our continent into various denominations.[3] Each defines the roles women should play in that specific cultural universe.

We can identify at least three European culture areas that have been transplanted in our denominational structures. One is the Mediterranean, brought to us in Italian and Spanish Catholicism. In this world view a highly ordered and stratified universe is acted out in a church hierarchy of all-male prelates. This is the original home of the "cult of the Virgin," a long tradition predating the Christian era, of young girls who see holy visions. The protection of women is expressed in reverence for the position of holiness in motherhood, and the honor of the family and lineage is upheld by all.

The movie *Light in the Piazza* points this up in terms of the simple and nonparticipatory role of women in an Italian Catholic household. An American mother is faced with the decision, according to *TV Guide,* of whether to put her beautiful twenty-six-year-old brain-injured daughter with the mind of a ten-year-old child in a special school or allow her to marry an Italian boy of a fine family. The ironic thing about the story is that the mother never reveals to the boy or his parents that her daughter is not perfectly normal. They are charmed with her childlike qualities and delighted for him to find such a good, fine, gentle, and sweet girl for a wife. What the plot seems to convey is that any intelligent and happy ten-year-old can fulfill the woman's role in a subculture holding a Mediterranean world view. Even the priest reports that she is "doing well in her instructions."

Southern England fell heir to this idealized version of woman along with the feudal adaptation of a plantation economy and the English vision of Christianity. The romantic images of women were accompanied by fortresses to keep arrows out and women in. This feudal-plantation system was transplanted to Virginia and South Carolina, and the "Southern lady" image has become part of a romantic American stereotype. The perpetuation of this image makes it difficult for women in the South even today to break loose and gain independence and professional equality.

A shortage of professional women job candidates exists in a region so long tied up in the notion of "Southern womanhood."

In addition to Mediterranean Christianity, we find another form of religion and world view in the people of the Middle European plains. One well-known representative is the Anglo-Saxon village in Germany, taken to the East Anglia region of England and onward to New England. The world view in this culture centers on the cooperative farming patterns needed to grow and harvest grain, and all adults participate equally in work activities. In this culture—brought to us by the Congregationalists, the Reformed peoples, the Baptists, the Amish, and some English Presbyterian groups—women have a great deal more stature under the Fatherhood of God (because they are all brothers and members of the priesthood of believers). At least the interaction within the church service differs, in that even in the early congregational meetings women were allowed to speak. And many women of this egalitarian tradition were among the early workers in the suffrage movement as well as spokeswomen for the present movement for Women's Liberation.

The third distinct religious variation in European denominations is that of the Celtic peoples, who occupied the fringe areas of Scotland, Wales, and Ireland. Since they are the original layer of habitation for the British Isles, the Celtic peoples—notably Scots and Welsh—retain many old traditional familial and tribal forms. It is the Celts who live scattered about in open farmsteads and keep cattle, whose religion is peopled by spirits and leprechauns as well as by God and the angels, and whose emphasis on kinship, the family, and clan gives the woman a pivotal place in the kinship and lineage.

Of course, after having been resettled on this continent for a hundred or two hundred years, most of the communal groups belonging to each culture area have been modified to adapt to new circumstances. But cultures are surprisingly persistent. We find Polish festivals in the streets of Chicago, St. Patrick's Day gatherings in Boston and New York. New England congregationalist villages are repeated in Kansas and Oregon, still cooperating as "brothers" to celebrate the Fourth of July. Lloyd Warner did an elegant study of one of these celebrations, Memorial Day in a New England city, in which the Puritans recreated their past in a parade of floats symbolically stating their values and world view.[4]

My own "people" for ethnographic study, the Scots Presbyterians whom I have described at length in chapter 3, migrated into the Southern Piedmont in the eighteenth century. They are mixed Celtic and Anglo-Saxon, originating in the southwest of Scotland where the Covenanters were active. In their present-day summer community, gathered together for religious conferences and family reunions, the world view of Calvinistic Presbyterian shouts out loud and clear. The aspect of this world view that pertains most directly to women is that of separation between the "flesh" and the "spirit." The "world" is associated with the city and with the worldly wickedness of drunkenness, sexual activity, gambling, and other licentiousness. The spiritual and good things can best be found in rural environments, in the old scattered open country neighborhood of the ancestors and in the traditional sacred grove, where Celtic rituals were held in communication with the spirits of the forest. Women take the children at the beginning of the summer into this idyllic community in the mountains, set up housekeeping, and the men visit at vacation times. The stated purposes are to give the children a safe place to spend the summers away from the environment of the city and to get together with the greater family. The unstated purpose is to have the children meet others of their own kind, so that later they will marry suitably and bring the grandchildren back every summer to continue the cycle.

In this group, as in much of general American society, women are assigned those tasks in the home and in the church that are associated with food-getting and child care. It might be inferred from comparative data in primitive societies that, because they are tied to menstruation and childbearing, women are presumably closer to the earth and to the flesh. These earthly tasks include cleaning the house, cooking and serving food, and handling children's bodily needs, such as diapering and bathing. In addition, women make arrangements for the preparing of food for family reunions and for all activities honoring the dead ancestors.

Men, meanwhile, read and study for the ministry, preach sermons, argue lawsuits, and read newspapers. Interestingly, the patterns of inheritance follow these social grooves, with sons inheriting their father's lawbooks and judicial robes, pulpit Bible, or tools of the business trade, while girls inherit their mother's jewelry, and the family sterling silver and china passes down the line from mother to daughter.

The most obvious expression of dichotomy between flesh and spirit is the separation of girls and boys for many activities of play and learning. Among adults this separation is particularly noticeable when applied to married couples. There are few mixed social occasions which men and women attend apart from their spouses during the entire period of sexual activity— a period of around twenty-five years. During this time married women attend the Ladies' Bible Class, sing in the choir and go to the Garden Club, and devote their professional energies to rearing their children "in the nurture and admonition of the Lord." After these years, of course, they have to devote considerable energy to being available for the long summer visits of their grown daughters with all the grandchildren.

The kin network and the family unity are based on this mother-daughter tie. Closest of kin are the children born from one mother. For instance, the term "half-brother" or "half-sister" is used for a person who had the same father but a different mother. All children born from one mother are considered full siblings and called "brother" or "sister" whether they had different fathers or not. This finding of the centrality of the mother-daughter bond is substantiated in the visiting patterns, in which daughters bring children home to visit their mother during the summer and in which the cousins who are the closest kin are the children of sisters because they always lived and played together in the summer.

Careful examination and comparison of ethnographic data from the major subcultural groups in the United States reveal that there is a strong tendency in them all to emphasize the centrality of the mother in transmitting the cultural heritage. This is pronounced in the Jewish family and we hear a great many jokes about it,[5] but it is apparent from the data that the central role of mother as socializer is shared by the major European traditions. It is within the kernel of the family unit that all the lore and laws of a people are learned. This kinship core becomes increasingly important in a people who live in scattered small-family bands and gather together only a few times a year.

If each subculture is to survive as an entity, the children must be taught the ways of the tribe and be brought together for ceremonial times so the sacred interpretations of the universe can be passed on.

If the mother waltzes off to medical school or goes into business apart from the family or decides to accept a research grant to the University of Zambia, how will the heritage persist? It is this central pivotal role of mother as maintainer of tradition within religious subcultures that makes such tightly knit groups resistant to changed roles for women.

The internal segments within U.S. Christianity are equally a part of the not-so-humorous "chicken soup syndrome" that operates to keep married women—and especially mothers—in their "proper place." Catholic schools crank out the slogan that "the man is head of the home, the woman is the heart." Protestants believe that "God couldn't be everywhere, so he made mothers." And while church pastors and counselors continue to worry about the children of working mothers, no one has thought much about the startling fact that a majority of all juvenile offenders have *fathers* who work.

It seems to me that the real structural problem to be solved is the one that allows only one role to the mother of a family. While in every tradition there seems to be a niche open for the spinster who chooses a career, there seems to be no acceptable slot for a woman with a family who pursues a career assertively. She does this against very real and very formidable negative social barriers. Allowing such a new role in a traditional culture threatens the continuation of that culture.

Liberation

Anthropologists are always accused of being conservative or even reactionary, because they sometimes paint a coherent picture of the workings of a culture but paint a dismal picture of the possibilities for social and cultural change. It is not my intention to be gloomy or to infer that these internal traditional groups are holding millions of women captive against their will. I simply intend to describe and define in the ethnographic sense what I see happening.

Applied anthropologists in community development programs have a history of going into a foreign country's culture with their brushes and trowels, defining the contours, grooves, or meanings and natural social groupings, and then attempting to implement government programs that will in fact bring about change without destroying lifeways and cultural arrangements.

I would like to think that a thorough understanding of religious-cultural learning of sex roles and of internal social groups could point the way to a well-designed program for liberation that would fit with cultural meanings and values.

Somehow, I am not optimistic about this as a possibility. World view *is* the explanation of the relation of the sexes to each other and to the natural world. Liberation from that is the equivalent of revolution, or at least the radical reformation of society.

What I do see as a possibility is the emergence of new cultural groups composed of those who have in some way broken loose from the old ways and are trying to live newly structured, liberated lives. Earlier, while toying with this social model, I named this group "maypole dancers." [6] John earlier postulated a new type of religion for these people, who include the intelligentsia—the academics, intellectuals, seminary students, and others who have made a conscious choice to attempt to break out and live by new rules with new loyalties. (Sometimes it seems like there are more of them than there are; the reason is that *they* are the ones writing the sociology books!)

Because no human can exist apart from a cultural group, the maypole dancers will have to invent new kin relationships, new rituals, new community forms within which to pass on their own world view of freedom and equality. Already we see these emerging in family-like communes, joint families, and informal marriages with "satellite" husbands or wives. We see new substitute kinship gatherings when groups of families who have taught at the same university or lived in the same town reestablish friendship at holiday times in preference to visiting blood kin. We see local congregations, particularly in the Unitarian movement, where children and parents and older adults, formerly members of assorted denominations, are attempting to establish rituals that communicate new possibilities in restructuring sex and age roles. Networks of families within church congregations go out to state parks for weekend camping, where a tribal *communitas* has new rules. Liberated rules allow cross-sex friendships, nondefensive adolescent and adult confrontations, and a modified extended family. Young children can have the benefit of ten or twelve older adopted siblings to look after them, and older children can express wonder at new infants. In these new scattered-and-gathered ideological communities, children see daddies cooking and washing and mommies reading lawbooks and writing lectures. They experience one-parent families who are a part of the total mosaic instead of some deviation from the norm. And, in a supportive community setting, when individuals fall back into older stereotyped behaviors, it is safe to reprimand, to insist on changes and reparations, without the danger of being labeled a weirdo or a freak.

Equality at the economic level is essential for women. Equal pay, time off for pregnancy, ability to establish credit and to own property are crucial to emancipation. Equality at the political level is also essential. Women must be able to vote and to hold office and must be equally represented according to numbers of population. These goals must be pursued in conjunction, however, with the goals of liberation at the level of family and kin-religious interaction. Goals at this level would include the freeing of women and men from religious socialization practices which stereotype the contribution of either sex. When the church teaches that women must stay at home and follow the "natural" law of having babies and rearing them in the faith, it is implicitly teaching that men are harnessed to the work world as "providers." And then neither one is free.

As humans we can never be free from cultural patterning and cultural persistency. As humans we do have the cognitive tools to analyze and, I hope, to change these invisible forces. Culture and learning have brought us as women into a position we are no longer willing to accept. Liberation is our word for creatively coming out of cultural shells into new possibilities.

John Comments

This is a difficult essay for me to comment upon. While I advocate the elimination of sex-role stereotypes and the liberation of women, I find that as a man I am continually a cause of the problem. I am more often a product of my socialization than

I would like to admit. Continually, for example, I find myself unconsciously using language I oppose, language which is a symbol of my own oppression in sex-role stereotyping, language which perpetuates the negative socialization of women. I'm committed in my head to new sorts of actions, and yet I often find myself reverting to the very patterns of behavior I deplore. But this confession is not my main point. I only thought it would be helpful to point out how strong the processes of socialization are in our lives and how men are in some ways oppressed just as women are. Both sexes need to be liberated, both resocialized. However, what I've been thinking most about is how Christian education in the church has often supported oppressive socialization patterns for women.

In 1972, four psychologists presented a report,[7] a ten-year study, on children and aggression. They looked at a wide variety of childhood experiences, including television viewing and church attendance. Their research discovered that similar experiences can have opposite effects on boys and girls. For example, they found that a heavy diet of television violence tended to make third-grade boys develop into aggressive eighteen-year-old men, while the same exposure for girls tended to make them develop into less aggressive women. As they pointed out, these findings do not support the contention that there are inborn differences in male and female behavior, but rather that socialization affects how boys and girls respond to the same experience— that is, boys are often encouraged and reinforced to act aggressively while girls are socialized otherwise. Thus television violence viewing for girls may actually have been a positively sanctioned social activity through which aggressive girls could express their aggression vicariously. (They also pointed out that there are far fewer aggressive females than males on television for girls to imitate.)

But of greater interest to me was their finding that the most consistent predictor of aggression in boys and girls was church attendance—that is, the greater the participation of parents and children in church, the more boys were aggressive and girls were not. Once again, this points to the role socialization in the church plays. The church may verbally teach that you are to love your enemies and turn the other cheek, but by the experiences they offer boys in the life of the church they may actually be teaching them the opposite.

What was interesting and troublesome to me was the implied extent to which the church is a mirror of society. Too often we socialize children into culturally defined roles, even though those roles may violate our own "teachings." It seems to me that it's about time we developed educational ministries in the church which endeavor to overcome sexism and empower persons to develop new understandings of life for both men and women. We ought to be freeing persons from limited roles and statuses and opening up new options for both men and women to exercise their full personhood in home, community, church, and world.

We need to do more justice to the contributions women, past and present, have made to church and society. Particularly, we need to increase the number of women who are ordained clergy. If we can change the role and status of women who provide leadership in the church, then perhaps we might be able to find a means for the resocialization of women and the overcoming of our negative sex-role stereotyping in the church. That won't be easy, for even though women have been ordained in some denominations for some time they are still not in significant numbers or in significant leadership positons to do what is necessary to change the socialization patterns in our churches. And I might point out that we will not adequately train women for this role until we add large numbers of women to our seminary faculties. We seem to have a lot of work to do before change will be realized.

Two books that I'd recommend to help us get started are Hewitt and Hiatt, *Women Priests, Yes or No,* and Stendahl, *The Bible and the Role of Women.*[8] When discussed with advocates of women's liberation, they can help the rest of us reconsider the problems of socialization and women in our theology, our church practice, and our church life. Religious education can and ought to assume the major responsibility for that task.

Meeting the sex and socialization problem head on will necessitate the resocialization of adults. That's the subject I've chosen for my next essay. But before you begin the next chapter, let me explain that it represents a personal, reflective, theological outgrowth of the conversations that inspired this book on religious socialization. Where it may lack objectivity, it possesses passion. I suppose I'll never become an uninvolved observer-describer of religious education. I have faith and I care about the church— so on occasion I preach. This is not meant to be an apology, only an explanation. In writing about sex and socialization, Gwen assumed a prophetic role. Now it's my turn.

Chapter 9

Reshaping Adults

John H. Westerhoff III

Our acquisition of motives, behaviors, beliefs, and attitudes does not end with the arrival of adulthood. Socialization is continuous through the life cycle.[1] Faced today with new challenges and a complex changing society, it is particularly important for us to explore the dynamics of adult socialization. How does the adult learn new behaviors in the middle of life?

Given the desire to explore socialization after childhood, we need to recognize its difficulty and limits. First, we must recognize the durable qualities of early childhood learning. Observe, for example, how difficult it is for most men and women to affirm or even deal with the women's liberation movement. Men will say, "It's okay, I guess, but not for *my* wife!" Later-life socialization often requires replacement of old learnings with new. New behaviors are required for new situations. At the same time, early socialization often makes the acceptance of change difficult.

Further, we must recognize that socialization necessitates a community as socializing agent. To produce lasting individual change in ourselves, by ourselves, is all but impossible. When no one around us believes change valuable, motivation for change is hard to establish. And even if, for a time, we do change, even if we do gain new understandings, perceptions, or behaviors, it is extremely difficult to maintain them if no community of significant others shares our views. It isn't enough to desire change in our behaviors, beliefs, and attitudes; we need to belong to a community which shares, supports, and encourages our desires.

Increasingly, persons are expressing their awareness that new roles are necessary for the faithful Christian in today's world.

The old individualistic roles of devoted spouse and parent, loyal institution-oriented church member, hard-working "breadwinner," cooperative neighborhood volunteer, and nationalistic patriotic citizen are no longer adequate. The complex interrelated social world in which we live, with its problems of racism, classism, sexism, war, poverty, injustice, nationalism, and imperialism (not to mention individual and corporate sin, principalities, and powers) demands that Christians affirm and acquire new understandings, roles, and behaviors.

However, it isn't enough to acknowledge this need. There are three things persons require before they are able to live differently. First, they must know what is expected of them in terms of both values and behaviors. Second, they must acquire the skills to fulfill those understandings and intentions. And third, they must desire to practice their new behaviors and pursue their new appropriate ends. The purposes, therefore, of adult socialization (or, better, resocialization) are to give persons new knowledge, skills, and motivation. Obviously, this cannot be accomplished without a supportive community of shared goals and understandings.

Change: Persons versus Groups

In that regard, I recall reading Seymour Sarason's book *The Culture of the School and the Problem of Change*.[2] It's the story of unsuccessful educational change, the analysis of a failure which went something like this: Single individual teachers were removed from their local schools (a subculture) and transported to a university (a different subculture) for a summer training session. There as individuals they were introduced to new knowledge, given new skills, and motivated to new actions. Then they were returned, as individuals, to their local schools, where the others did not share their new knowledge, skills, or motivation. Soon they reverted to their old ways or, frustrated, left teaching convinced that change would never occur.

After reading that book, I concluded we've done the same sort of thing in the church. How often have we enticed local clergy or lay people to a seminary or conference for new knowledge, skills, and motivation and then returned them to their churches, only to watch them revert to old ways or become alienated from their congregation and on occasion leave the church in frustration? In neither case were they able to create or maintain change —the very reason we encouraged them to attend our workshop.

I now believe it would have been wiser to have brought them in groups, so that they could have gained new knowledge, skills, and motivations through the establishment of a supportive community. We cannot permanently change our beliefs, attitudes, and behaviors alone; we require a supportive community in which to learn and practice our new knowledge and abilities, as well as have our motivation for change encouraged and sustained. If we are concerned about the resocialization of adults for new social understandings, roles, and behaviors, we cannot any longer plan educational programs for single individuals. It is essential that we conduct our educational efforts with and for groups of individuals. Therefore I suggest we shift our attention from seeking to help individuals acquire new knowledge, abilities, and motivations to aiding in the formation of supportive communities with knowledge, abilities, and motivations. To state my proposition somewhat differently, religious education should focus its endeavors on the formation and continuing life of small groups that can and will become communities of changed persons with a common shared faith.

Needless to say, I find the current thinking of personal-evangelistic movements highly questionable. They typically say, "If you want society to change, you need only to change individuals. Stay away from evangelizing structures. By changing individuals, you build the necessary foundation for changing structures and groups."[3] I find that position difficult to defend. People change when they unite with a community which lives and supports a style of life different from their previous style of life. Unless we can reform and renew the structures and corporate life of churches, we will not be able to effectively aid individuals become more Christian—that is, unless you believe that the church as it is represents the perfect Christian community.

True conversion is not essentially an individualistic act. It results from contact with a community. Individual conversion is nothing more than a passing emotional outburst unless it is sustained within a community. Conversion and nurture are both social phenomena, just as socialization is. Conservative evangelistic movements (represented by much of "Key 73") with their emphasis on soul-saving do indeed encourage persons to become active church members. But "converts" of such culturally influenced movements are not likely to seek churches which can nurture radically changed lives committed to the Christ of social and personal justice, liberation, and peace.

A major contribution of socialization theory is the importance of communities of shared meaning. Of course, individual behavior and thought are not determined by such communities. Individuals act and react. But they always do so within a community; they also require a community to sustain them. That is why we can know a lot about a person simply by asking: To what groups do you belong?

If we desire to resocialize adults for new understandings, roles, and behaviors, we need to build new congregations. That means social change, group change, institutional change. In that regard, it would be well to reflect on an observation of Columbia University Professor Amitai Etzioni. Once, he recounted, there was an electrical shortage in New York. The university mounted a major educational campaign to encourage students and faculty to "save a watt." It just didn't work. Changing individuals' behaviors through education is difficult. Then, he says, they had the janitors remove half the light bulbs. That saved electricity, and gradually students and faculty changed their behavior of turning on lights. (It's just useless to turn on lights which do not work.) New social structures can enable us to change our behavior. Perhaps we need to cease talking of renewal in the church through education and speak about reformation through structural change.

The Church and the Culture

Most of us speak too glibly of "being in Christ." The history of the saints in every age is the history of men and women who, as "persons in Christ," found themselves continually involved in the uneasiness of radical change and social scandal. The early Christian community, humanly speaking, would have been wise to remain quietly in seclusion. Instead it became involved in conflicts with the dominant culture, conflicts which grew sharper until they resulted in persecution. Some people in the church today are believers in the Madison Avenue image of size and popularity. If a church has thousands of adherents and is increasing in numbers, they say it must be successful. There are those who have noticed that the conservative evangelical churches in the United States are growing in the same proportions that main-line liberal churches are losing members. These folk conclude that the conservative evangelical churches must be doing something right; some even say it is proof they are more religious. "Seek, therefore, to adopt the ways of these churches" is their recommendation. But what such advocates seem to ignore is that in spite of much pious rhetoric and biblical recitation these conservative evangelical churches may only be popular because they mirror and bless the dominant culture's beliefs, attitudes, and values. Typically, such churches neglect to ask the painful question: Isn't the community which claims Jesus as Lord to be a social witness against the culture until the full realization of God's reign? Churches which do that will always be small and rarely be popular. All they will ever be able to claim is faithfulness.

When thinking about the church, we easily get confused. We ignore the fact that we are socialized into our beliefs, attitudes, and values. Consider how the Southern church theologically supported slavery. Consider how churches have supported competition in economics, individualism in politics, and paternalism in social service. The church has often been a cultural chameleon instead of the people of God. Of course, it's not easy to be otherwise. There are many powerful forces of socialization in society which affect our lives. The church is but one.

Never forget that the culture calls upon its religious institutions to be communities of cultural continuity. As such, churches are to conserve the understandings and ways of life of the society by giving them religious sanctions. But God calls upon the church to be a community of cultural change. As such, churches are to prophetically judge society's understanding and way of life, just as they are to act on behalf of other understandings and ways. To be in Christ is to be in the world, but not of the world. When the church easily adopts and blesses the culture, it is being "of the world." Some days it is difficult to know which we have done.

We are called to be "free in Christ"—that is, to be obedient only to the will of God. But the tragedy is that we can so easily unconsciously identify the will of our culture with God's will. Of course, that difficulty will always be with us, for the church can never be free of its culture, but it can strive to be otherwise. And we know that in history it not only has often done so, but it has been successful in effecting significant cultural change.

Like persons, the church is both the product of and the producer of culture. To realize the first is to confess our sinfulness; to affirm the latter is to live in God's grace. In any case, the church faces an emotional tension between being product and producer. The Christian life is not a destination reached at some magic moment identified as conversion or confirmation; it is rather a journey. Discipleship is not something that can be learned once and for all time. It is a permanent apprenticeship in the school of faith, a way of life which can easily cause us anxiety.

Recall the Grand Inquisitor who reminds Jesus that people do not want freedom; they want to be told, they want security, they want to be like others and liked by others. And, as he reminds Jesus, if I give the word they will kill you, and do so in the name of religion. I suppose the church always gets panic-stricken from fear of the turmoil that Christ creates when he comes on the scene. The truth is that the Christ is unwelcome to each of us. To be asked to live in constant tension with our culture is not a life easily accepted. And to change our lives is even more disturbing. Yet Christ's call and gift of freedom is freedom from the confines of the past and present for a new, not entirely clear, future—freedom from the binding power of life as it is to life as it might become. Neither is necessarily enticing.

Aware of the dominating power of culture and the powerful forces of socialization, it is difficult to understand how the gospel has survived without being wholly adapted and transformed by the culture. It is a miracle that it has not only survived but continuously called forth a remnant to live in its power. Thus it is that the church has been a revolutionary influence on culture and history. And it has been most faithful to its calling when it was performing that role.

The Christian Future

From the first century to the present, to be "in Christ" has been to be liberated from the prison of life as it is. It is to be free to change our lives so that we are no longer bound by the past or by our previous socialization into beliefs, attitudes, and behaviors. Mature Christians with a vision of the reign of God and the hope that affirms the coming of that vision are able to stand back and judge both their own and society's present perspectives, beliefs, attitudes, and values. Such persons are aware and emotionally sensitive to the needs of all humankind, are motivated by a concern and commitment to justice, and are inner-directed in their behavior.

To be in Christ is to have faith in persons and the possibility of shalom. It is to be involved in those sociopolitical activities which aim for peace, harmony, justice, liberation, health, equality, wholeness, and fulfillment for humankind and nature. To be in Christ is to live a particular life-style, a life-style founded upon a particular faith. Regretfully, we have a tendency to swing from a concern for living a particular sort of life to a concern for faith. But both life-style and faith are essential to be a Christian. As a matter of fact, in the final analysis they cannot be separated.[4]

When the church tries to proclaim its faith only in words, it dies from hypocrisy. When the church tries to communicate its faith only through experience, it dies from abstractness. When the church tries to live out its faith only through actions, it dies from rootlessness. When the church, as a community in history, unites its heritage—its memory and vision—with reflected-upon experience and planned action around social and personal issues, it lives. Such life is expressed in the constant grappling for solidarity among telling the good news, teaching persons how to live that good news, and enabling the community to act out that good news in the world.

Such faith is generated and communicated by a witnessing community of believers. The business of the church is neither the promotion of a special style of individual life called piety nor ministering to what some call the "religious needs" of people. The church is rather called and challenged to be a historical agency, under the lordship of Christ, acting in the world to the end that God's will be done and his kingdom come.

It is true, as Pascal once said, that "one Christian is no Christian." It may be chauvinistic to say, "To have God as our father it is necessary to have the church as our mother," but it points to a profound truth. If we are to be the children of God, we need a community to convert us and a community to nurture us, that we may nurture our children in the faith. We simply cannot be Christian or bring up Christian children by ourselves. We can't remain Christians alone. Not in our modern world.

For this reason, if no other, the local church is not and never will be obsolete. Without local communities of faith, the Christian faith can never be acquired, sustained, or communicated. But like the New Testament communities that carried the gospel, they must be aimed outward. They cannot exist for themselves but must live and act for others, particularly those who are the poor, the outsiders, the oppressed, the hurt, and the needy. Christians are called to celebrate a vision of the world as God intends it to be (new knowledge), to tell of that vision through word-in-deed (new skills), and to act upon that vision (new motivations). We do that by belonging to a world-oriented, socially active, supportive community of faith.

From my perspective, the structures and activities of the church can only be justified insofar as they enable the community of faith to become a historical voluntary association through which God frees persons and groups from the enslavement to all those powers, principalities, institutions, and practices which would dehumanize personkind. Such a church is a community of shalom.

A New Resource

Recall that shalom is a common Hebrew word of greeting and parting. But its meaning runs far deeper than mere formality. Shalom is whole community, liberation and justice, harmony and peace, fullness of life. In a sense it is a vision—the reign of God. In Jesus, the shalom of God is present among us as a gift, for which we are called to respond and act.

Shalom, however, also refers to a new adventure in Christian education, the Shalom Curriculum [5]—an educational approach that takes the vision of shalom as its unifying principle.

To call this significantly different educational endeavor a curriculum may be confusing; for many people, a curriculum means a package of printed materials to be used by teachers in a classroom. In this case, however, the word curriculum refers to the course to be run, the route of a journey, or the direction of our travels. It implies numerous and diverse planned efforts throughout the total life of a congregation that are consistent with the goal of shalom.

At a time when many are depressed by the inadequacies of their educational efforts, the Shalom Curriculum points to the possibility of an alternative future. That statement is not meant to sound grandiose or utopian; it does intend to communicate a hope and a desire.

For some time many people have been seeking better ways to establish the Bible as the central focus of their educational mission. At the same time, others have been searching for new ways to unify formal teaching with other aspects of the church's life and ministry.

The Shalom Curriculum responds to both quests. By aiming for shalom, it grounds its goals in the very heartbeat of the biblical faith. And by taking the total life of a congregation as the context for education, it makes possible a positive program to enable and equip children, young people, and adults to be faithful to the gospel. It affirms, further, the need for local churches to plan their own educational ministries. Curriculum needs to be built by those who use it! An essential aid in this endeavor is *Signs of Shalom* by Edward A. Powers. It is an exciting, practical guidebook—a basic resource for planners in local churches.[6]

Challenge to Church Educators

The church is required continually to judge and reorder its life so that its people can be captured by a vision of God's kingdom and inspired and supported in ways which enable them to join God in his history-making. That struggle for reformation is what I mean by adult resocialization. There may have been a time when persons could simply be brought up as Christians, never knowing themselves as anything else. There may have been a time when the church was naturally a community of Christian faith. That just isn't true today. A reformation that builds new faith communities is essential. The resocialization of adults into the Christian faith is also essential. The two go together, for without new faithful communities we will not be able to resocialize adults; without resocialized adults we will be without the necessary faithful communities. We cannot do one unless at the same time we do the other.

Adult resocialization in the Christian faith can only take place in a particular sort of community. It is a community which has conscious goals, aims, purposes, objections, and conviction. It is a community of converted persons—those who have had their lives turned around—who, being aware of the life they were unconsciously socialized into as children and the required life of a disciple, have consciously chosen the latter and committed themselves to live and act in a supporting community which shares their understandings and commitment. It is a community with shared experiences, self-understanding, and vision. It is a community which has a faith it wants to tell and do and is thus willing to sacrifice all the world's praise and benefits on behalf of a life of faithfulness. The church has in moments of history been that sort of community, and men and women have left everything behind to give their individual lives to its corporate action in history as an agent of God's kingdom-building.

Only as we unite the inner and outer search of persons with the quest for self-knowledge and social justice will we be faithful to our Lord. Bound by a common vision and a commitment to a new future for personkind and nature, the Christian is liberated from the prison of what is and motivated by what yet can be. No longer can we Christians consider ourselves victims of history. Rather we are to know ourselves as molders of history. No longer can we perceive life as a matter of adaptation. Rather we are to understand life as transformation. Such perceptions are as possible as any other. It is simply a matter of deciding what communities we will join and commit our lives to. For it is within such chosen communities that we are socialized and reshaped.

If as adults we have come to realize the bankruptcy of our lives as we have been socialized to live them, then it is time for us to unite with others who share our desire for new life and so live together as to resocialize ourselves into new understandings and ways.

Socialization is not only for children. Today we are in a period when many aspects of enculturation which have been blessed by the church are recognized as corrupt. The times call for a new reformation, a reformation that will bring into being new communities of faith where the resocialization of adults can take place. Only then will the church be able once again to nurture the next generation in the faith.

We need a revival, not of the sort supported by some evangelical conservative or fundamentalistic movement but a revival

Chapter 10

Continuity and Change in Human Culture [1]

Gwen Kennedy Neville

Since the dawn of the species, every human being has been born into a world of change. At the same time, persons have experienced a world which is also continuous and stable. Both change and persistency are built into the unfolding order of the natural and social universe.

How can we explain these two seemingly contradictory threads of life? What are the dynamics for learning one's particular culture? How is it possible for individuals to adopt new ways of ordering their lives? How do individuals and cultures change— and how do they continue? These are the questions that trouble the anthropologist who is looking at contemporary America, itself a collage of change and tradition.

As an anthropologist, I have observed numerous mobile families who appear to be in constant flux. At the same time I have witnessed pockets of ethnic culture deeply rooted and fixed in European and Latin American tradition. Any attempt to analyze these phenomena is complicated by my own involvement with one of America's multiple subcultures. I, too, have been born into a world view and have been taught a "right" way to order life.

But out of this confusion of trying to understand social change comes reassuring data from evolutionary studies. They state loudly: "Remember, the human species has evolved in a process of orderly change over a period of many millions of years." Culture, embodied in human society, is a relative newcomer to the scene and takes up only a tiny shaded layer on the time chart of the biological universe. Yet it operates according to the same systematic expected series of unfolding processes. Remains of past civilizations recorded in pottery and tools testify to gradual changes over time, even in the most "traditional" cultures. A certain style of vase or water jar appears in the archaeological record, gains popularity, becomes more and more numerous, and then gradually disappears over a period of several thousand years. Although it is impossible to dig up the remains of social life and religion, we can be certain that these aspects of that particular civilization were also slowly changing.

An individual's lifetime is far too short to use as a measure of gradual change. Within the brief space of a half century a person lives and acts out special goals and dreams within a particular cultural system, a cultural system which will influence to a great degree what those goals and dreams will be. We witness every day the conflicting goals of various subcultural systems, each attempting to preserve its separateness and identity.

Human beings in every subculture are struggling to retain a continuous, orderly tradition to pass on to their children. If we hope to live in this complex urban world, it is essential that we begin to look seriously and realistically at the nature of cultural systems and the ways in which humans learn their culture. Sensitized by these understandings, we may decide to modify our own attempts at innovation and intervention. We may also understand somewhat more clearly the phenomenon of *change* and its relationship to continuity.

Cultural Transmission

The basic learning of a culture and its appropriate behavior takes place in very early years of life. It is a process which begins with the handling of the infant immediately following birth. In our own society this is taken over by the hospital nurse, who washes and wraps the infant and separates the child from its mother for three days or more. While many cultures assign early days of care and feeding to the mother alone, who nurses the infant at the breast, the American hospital replaces the mother with a plastic crib and the breast with a rubber nipple. The infant is receiving important impulses about the cultural world from these sequences.

Specific subcultural patterns of behavior are learned after the mother and infant have left the hospital and gone home. Arrangement of the furniture communicates values about the use of space. The presence or absence of siblings or of an extended family in the house will influence the availability and the allocation of space. An only child in a wealthy family learns different meanings than does one of twelve children in a big-city apartment. Time gains meanings, also, and these are inherent in the sequence of feedings, holding, and cuddling. Body movements communicate meanings about the nature of touch and the closeness of persons. Sounds made by the mother communicate either comfort or distaste about excretory functions. A mother's sounds also reinforce certain sounds made by the infant. In this way "ma-ma" may start out as a meaningless jargon but become a symbol of great intensity. Because parents carry in their heads a set of cultural instructions which inform them about the appropriate meanings of time, space, and language symbols, they communicate these to their offspring through their behaviors.

As a baby grows, interaction takes place between the child and a widening circle of others. In every event participated in, a particular order and spacing of actions is appropriate. And each type of event—play, school, sports, church—has its own internal structuring of behaviors, all of which an individual learns slowly as a part of a culture. From a behavioral point of view, "culture" can be defined as the sum of all these events. Thus a culture consists of agricultural activities, trading and marketing activities, the groupings and interactions of kinsmen, activities related to governing and social control, and those events and activities of a religious or ceremonial nature. Even though each type of event has its own specific patterns or prescribed interaction, the individuals sharing a culture also share a world view and meanings. Therefore, a person's patterns of behavior will be coupled with those of the fellow culture-carriers. For example, think how good it feels to relax with people you know well and who agree with you. This relaxedness is a result of sharing cultural understandings.

By the time a person has reached adulthood, he or she has internalized a whole package of cultural meanings, signals, and symbols which indicate "right" ways of doing things and "appropriate" ways to behave. Anyone who doubts the tenacity of early learned patterns of space need only take a bus ride in an Arab country to experience culturally defined distance of individuals. An American is often overwhelmed by closeness that seems natural to that country's population. Cross-cultural definitions of time are discovered daily by the visitor to Latin America, where "after lunch" may mean four thirty in the afternoon. And as for the ordering of action within events, the order of worship in a high church Episcopal service proceeds along patterns that are comfortable to the person whose internal timing has been conditioned to liturgy. This same order, however, is unfamiliar and seems stilted to the visiting friend from a Pentecostal denomination. At the same time, if the Episcopalian were to visit a Pentecostal testimonial service or one for faith healing, he might be the one who felt uncomfortable.

Time, space, and order of behavior are always learned within the context of a human group. This group includes the family and extends into a person's cultural network, taking the form we know as human community.

Communities, Cycles, and Human Beings

Human communities in earlier times were easily distinguishable because "a culture" and "a community" were synonymous among primitive peoples and among peasant societies. In other words, the world view learned in childhood was carried out in every form of activity engaged in by adults, including even the way houses and villages were arranged. Furthermore, these arrangements in the hunting and gathering societies were closely connected to seasonal cycles of availability or scarcity of game. In agricultural peoples, seasons for planting and harvesting influenced arrangements in other aspects of the culture—that is, all types of human activities and events revolved around the crops and their success.

It is much more difficult to identify the boundaries of "a culture" or "a community" within a highly complex industrial society. Urban America is a melee of subcultures and overlapping communities. Because the anthropologist assumes that humans continue to be organized along biosocial lines, the researcher looks for meaningful communities within the social networks of interrelated families which share a world view and a learned culture pattern. Using this model, communal gatherings and important religious celebrations, along with kinship and occupation, define the dimensions of a person's communities.

Communal gatherings, and special events in a person's life

cycle, define a shared set of understandings, of world view. Within the gatherings for these communal celebrations, individuals revitalize their beliefs, reestablish interaction with kin and meaningful friends, and in general get new fuel for enacting cultural patterns that may have weakened and become dormant. We say we are "renewed" after a vacation or a church conference. In fact, we are. We have gained new reinforcement for the values and meanings we wish to enact during the regular cycle of everyday life.

Keeping and Changing Cultural Ways

All this talk of the learning, teaching, and reenacting of shared meanings may make culture sound as if it has humans locked into a sequence that is unchanging. This cannot possibly be true, of course, for we have already mentioned the evidence for constant change. Even within a lifetime, children grow up to be different from their parents, and a denomination today is different from the same one fifty years ago. Humans change slowly, however; and when they do, the new ways are taken in through cultural filing systems that classify and catalog all new material. New ideas come through a screen formed by culture. New behaviors come gradually, within grooves that have been established for the earliest years of life.

The community changes, too, but according to these same rules, for it is made up of human beings, and ritual behavior is so persistent because it is very close to the center of those values which give meaning to every other area of life. The ordering of ritual may act as the one positive and familiar reinforcing event in an otherwise busy and chaotic world of the city. In church at a worship service the individual experiences anew the old familiar patterns and time sequences, the familiar use of space, the comforting sounds of music and rhythms heard many times before. Sitting with closest family and friends, renewing early behaviors and meanings, a person finds a reestablishment of lost order and forgotten innocence. He or she emerges with the necessary fortification to launch into another week.

Those who find meaning in the folk mass, known to Protestants as "contemporary worship," are among a layer of the population who have transferred their loyalties over time to changing forms and to change itself. Many of these change-oriented adults learned as children to expect a universe that is not limited to any one single world view. The newer forms of worship have meaning for some. For others a more deeply rooted tradition continues to give significance to life.

Tension between the subtle processes of change and the maintenance of set order keeps the human social group in that state of constant flux necessary for life. This dynamic equilibrium is the result and the basis of life itself. One goal in life maintaining itself is to preserve ongoing patterns. A second and equally important goal for life is a responsiveness to the environment. This responsiveness is necessary to adapt for survival. Without both persistence and flexibility the organism, or the organic community, will not remain viable.

An Observer's Benediction

So the anthropologist returns to the original questions of change and persistence. Somehow, when seen as two elements within culture, neither change nor tradition seems quite as frightening. Change sometimes seems to get out of control, and its disciples become conservative in their liberalism. A folk saying puts this condition aptly: "It is just as bad to have your window stuck open as to have it stuck closed. Either way you can't use the window."

Just as change is never all good, tradition can't be all bad. Basic traditional cultural ways are essential to the ongoing life of every person. Even as new ideas are adopted into old grooves, old ideas are preserved with the flavor of new ones that enrich and enhance.

Human beings, social change, tradition-keeping, urban communities—to this observer, all look like natural processes in the unfolding order of life.

John Comments

Gwen and I have probably discussed change more than any other subject. As an anthropologist, she affirms a biological image of slow, continuous evolution-like change. I'm not sure whether I really disagree with her or not. The issue is difficult to sort out. But since its consequences are so profound, the discussion should be aired. So let me share another point of view, best represented by Robert Nisbet in his book *Social Change and History*.[2]

Nisbet is also a social scientist, but when he looked, from a different perspective, at what he calls the dominant metaphor of change in Western thought, he concluded that we have too easily accepted that metaphor as true. He goes on to maintain that while change obviously does occur, change is not natural, constant, normal, or evolutionary. The law of history, he suggests, is not change but fixity. We might, he points out, say with Newton that every body continues in its state of rest or uniform motion in a straight line unless it is compelled to change that state by forces impressed upon it. Fixity, then, is the important point of departure for the study of social change. Conventional wisdom disagrees with Nisbet, and yet, as I've often pointed out, nothing is more obvious than the conservative bent of human behavior, the manifest desire to preserve, to hold, to fix and keep stable. Anyone who has ever attempted to initiate social change knows the immense power of habit, custom, and tradition. Nisbet, therefore, suggests that a law might read: "When it is not necessary to change it is necessary not to change." Of course, fixity unpunctured by change is as unlikely in the world of actuality as is change unpunctuated by fixity. To that extent the argument is ridiculous.

Finally Gwen and I agree; so do we and Professor Nisbet. The issue is which—continuity or change—do we affirm as dominant or most usual in history? My argument is that the way Gwen talks about the problem gives the impression that change takes place much too naturally. As a result, those who agree are likely to sit back and wait for change to occur. That worries me because I desire change. However, if you assume, as I do, that change will not occur unless we act to make it do so, then we will spend our time and energy devising the means by which we can act to effect that change.

True, both continuity and change are part of history. Gwen and I agree on that. More important than that agreement is our different belief of which is dominant or *more* usual. I'm opting for emphasizing that continuity is stronger, more dominant and natural in history. Therefore we need consciously, purposefully, and continuously to act so as to force social change to occur. If we so act, change will result. Interestingly, we even agree on that.

Finally, only our perspectives differ. Gwen tends to take the long historical look and is more relaxed about planning and anxiously attempting to bring about change. I take a shorter look and am more anxious to do something immediately so as to effect change now. I believe that the two positions in tension are healthy. Mine stimulates people to act; Gwen's helps them to stay cool and not lose their hope. What is most important is that everyone concerned about intentional religious socialization participates in that discussion and its implications.

That's one point I'd like to make; the other is very different. It might seem as if I'm only interested in change. Not true. In terms of purposeful religious socialization, I'm also interested in how we maintain continuity with our religious tradition when confronted by the diversity of secular traditions which surrounds us, each desiring that we change to adopt theirs.

Lynn Meloy, a student at Harvard, wrote a term paper which explored that issue in a fascinating manner.[3] I'd like to share her thesis. Earlier she had engaged in an ethnographic study of Hillel meetings with Reformed Jews in Cambridge, Massachusetts. She discovered a fascinating aspect of these meetings—namely, the use of controversy within a particular environment as a means for sustaining the Jewish understanding and way of life. Jews, as a minority population, have always struggled in the United States to maintain their identity while assimilating some aspects of the dominant American culture. They needed to find a means whereby they could be exposed to different views while not diluting their identity—in fact, while strengthening it. Already grounded in a tradition which emphasized scholarship, it seemed natural to introduce controversial discussion into their gatherings.

She observed that at each Hillel meeting they invited a guest who represented a position they did not share. After listening carefully to a presentation of this person's views, they engaged in a discussion of its merits. Each evening resulted in a community's supportive grappling with an outsider. As they aided each other through friendly argument with their guest, they learned how to account for other viewpoints and yet maintain their own frame of reference. They could show respect for the other's viewpoint and without extreme emotion support their own. Thus they sustained their common understanding of life and way of life.

Ms. Meloy concluded that in this case "controversy" was being used as an effective *means* for maintaining Jewish identity. We usually don't think of the importance of such organizations and their meetings for religious socialization; even less do we consider using controversy as an aid to identity formation. I'd like to suggest that we do consider such questions, for continuity as well as change is important.

That brings me to a final comment. As I have used the word culture in this book, I have understood it as an organized way of life, based on a common tradition and conditioned by a common environment. As such, every culture has common beliefs and a common way of life. Consequently, culture and religion are intricately bound together. The relation between them is always a two-sided one: conservative and dynamic—that is, a people's way of life influences their approach to religion and their religious attitude influences their way of life.

Religion normally exerts a conservative influence on culture. Nevertheless it also provides a dynamic means of social change, for if the impulse to change comes from a source which claims "transcendent authority" there is tremendous power. What I'm implying is that religious institutions have power—more than they suppose—both negative and positive (in terms of social change). The whole history of culture shows that we humans have a natural tendency to seek a "religious" foundation for our social way of life. For this reason culture becomes unstable when it loses its "spiritual" base.

Christopher Dawson in 1947 gave the Gifford Lectures. He entitled them *Religion and Culture*. In his chapter on religion and cultural change, he wrote:

Any religious movement which adopts a purely critical and negative attitude to culture is a force of destruction and disintegration which mobilized against itself the healthiest and most constructive elements of society—elements which can by no means be dismissed as worthless from the religious point of view. On the other hand, the identification of religion with the particular cultural synthesis which has been achieved at a definite point of time and space by the action of historical forces is fatal to the universal character of religious truth. It is indeed a kind of idolatry.[4]

The marriage of religion and culture is fatal to both partners. If religion is too tied to the social order, it loses its spiritual character. If religion is too estranged from the social order, it loses its transcendent power.

Religious institutions are called to live in the realization of this tension and precarious balance. Continuity and change appear to be essential aspects of both religion and culture. Religious socialization and resocialization provide the Christian educator with a unique perspective from which to understand and use both in evaluating and planning educational ministries. I further believe that intentional religious socialization suggests important means for evolving an alternative future for the Christian church, its educational mission, and its ministry. These essays have attempted to provide a stimulus and aid in that important reforming and renewing process.[5]

Religious Education and Culture—
Readings and Resources

Following are course outlines and their bibliographies for two seminars related to religion, education, and culture, one taught by John and one by Gwen. Those who are interested in the further study of the issues presented in the book may find them helpful.

More important for us are comments from our readers. When John wrote *Values for Tomorrow's Children,* he encouraged readers to write of their criticism, comments, concerns, and questions. Many did. We also encourage you to write. Only together will we be able to frame a viable alternative future.

Obviously, we did not intend this book to provide answers, but we did hope it would open up relevant questions and stimulate new responses. We encourage you to join us in our continuing search because, while these are disturbing days for Christian education and the church, they are also days of peculiar hope.

Human beings in groups and as individuals possess the latent ability to make great creative leaps forward and to adapt in new and useful ways, but this potential may be unused until a new and stressful survival situation occurs. When pushed to change and grow or become extinct, people will call upon every possible capability for the solution of the problem.

We have attempted here not to present absolutes or solutions but only to provide insights that may spark new ways of marshaling the resources for creative problem-solving within church education. We hope that both the people of the "lifeboat" and the people of the "maypole" will find a fresh way of looking at old realities within their worlds and some means for assisting in the transmission of those realities from one generation to another.

Anthropology of Religion

(Seminar at Emory University, Winter 1973)

Gwen Kennedy Neville

Texts

William A. Lessa and Evon Z. Vogt (eds.), *Reader in Comparative Religion: An Anthropological Approach.*

W. Lloyd Warner, *The Family of God: A Symbolic Study of Christian Life in America.*

Samuel S. Hill, Jr., et al., *Religion and the Solid South.*

Course Outline

Week 1: Introduction to the Course. Goals, requirements, etc. The discipline of anthropology, methods and viewpoint.

Week 2: Anthropological Approaches to the Study of Religion. History, theories, various points of attack.

Read: Lessa and Vogt, pp. 1–93. Also see: Michael Banton (ed.), *Anthropological Approaches to the Study of Religion* (selected articles); look especially at Clifford Geertz, in Banton and in Donald R. Cutler (ed.), *The Religious Situation.* Also Neville article, "Human Beings and Social Change," in *Colloquy* (Sept. 1972).

Week 3: Symbolic Expressions, Myths, and the Natural Universe. The concept of "world view," cognitive categories, "etic and emic."

Read: Lessa and Vogt, pp. 106–238. Also see: Dorothy Lee, "Codification of Reality," in her *Freedom and Culture.* Also her article in *Colloquy* (Sept. 1972).

Week 4: Symbolic Enactments—Space and Time Dimensions of Social Reality.

Read: Warner, *The Family of God.*

Week 5: Rites and Rituals. Seasonal cycles, life-crisis cycles. Rites of passage and rites of intensification. Interaction, behavior, and ceremonials.

Read: Lessa and Vogt, pp. 323–372. Also see: Eliot D. Chapple and Carleton Coon, "Rites of Passage" and "Rites of Intensification," in *Principles of Anthropology;* Arnold van Gennep, *Rites of Passage;* and Victor W. Turner, *The Ritual Process: Structure and Anti-Structure.*

Week 6: Economic Base, Religion, and Social Control.

Read: Lessa and Vogt, pp. 381–493. Also see: Roy A. Rappaport, *Pigs for the Ancestors: Ritual in the Ecology of a New Guinea People,* on ecological balances.

Week 7: Religious Responses to Change. Revitalization movements, messianic movements, "cargo cults."

Read: Lessa and Vogt, pp. 496–531. Additional readings on Pan-Indianism, Black Muslims, American revivalism of the nineteenth century, the "Jesus people," the women's liberation movement, etc.

Week 8: Religion and the Transmission of Culture. The dynamics of enculturation and cultural persistence as expressed in community form and value learning.

Read: Hill, pp. 57–121. Also see: *Colloquy* (Sept. 1972) articles by Bruno Bettelheim, Margaret Mead, and the Anthropological Group Interview. Also Neville, "Religious Socialization of Women in U.S. Subcultures," in Alice Hageman (ed.), *Sexist Religion and Women in the Churches: No More Silence.*

Week 9: American Ethnic and Regional Religious Communities.

Read: Hill, pp. 24–56 and 122–208. Also see: Neville, "Ceremonials and the Social Network," and Westerhoff, "Religion for the Maypole Dancers." Other suggestions: Mary McCarthy, *Memories of a Catholic Girlhood;* Dan Greenburg, *How to Be a Jewish Mother;* Willie Morris, *North Toward Home;* John Hostetler and Gertrude Enders Huntington, *Children in Amish Society;* and David Schulz, *Coming up Black: Patterns of Ghetto Socialization.*

Week 10: Seminar papers and summary of course.

For term paper: Choose one of the following and complete the assignment, using a specific community, culture, ethnic group, church, or small society as an observational field. Your data may be gleaned from first-hand ethnographic fieldwork or from library material—the best data come from a combination of these two techniques.

1. Examine the arrangements within this community relating to economics (making a living), family and kin, and maintaining social control (government). Now relate each of these to the "world view" of this small interacting unit.

2. Do a detailed interactional analysis of the ritual occasions of the group you have selected. Show how time and space use reflect meanings and values. Indicate the way in which these ritual events reflect or relate to the social structure of the present and future universe of these people.

3. Look at child-rearing practices (religious socialization). Piece together the interwoven values and beliefs that are being transmitted through interaction within daily routines and ritual occasions.

4. Make a detailed study of the calendrical cycle as affected by environment and production. Now superimpose on this a study of the cycle of religious festivals and events and show the ways in which these two cycles interface.

Appendix 2

The Church as a Learning Community

(An Introduction to Religious Socialization,
Harvard Divinity School, Fall 1972)

John H. Westerhoff III

Session 1: Methods and Approaches.

Film: *Beggar at the Gate.*

Session 2: Religion and Culture.

Readings: Christopher Dawson, *Religion and Culture,* or
Samuel S. Hill, Jr., et al., *Religion in the Solid South;* Charles H.
Anderson, *White Protestant Americans: From National Origins to
Religious Group;* Paul Tillich, *Theology of Culture;* Thomas Luck-
mann, *Invisible Religion;* Peter L. Berger, *The Sacred Canopy;*
or Annemarie De Waal Malefijt, *Religion and Culture.*

Session 3: Socialization.

Film: *Cultural Patterns and Infant Regulation.*

Readings: Choose from one of the following: *Autobiography
of Malcolm X;* Willie Morris, *North Toward Home;* Mary McCarthy,
Memories of a Catholic Girlhood; Norman Podhoretz, *Making It;*
or Garry Wills, *Bare Ruined Choirs: Doubt, Prophecy and Radical
Religion.*

Session 4: Socialization: Religion and Religious Institutions.

Readings: Robert W. Lynn and Elliott Wright, *The Big Little
School;* John Hostetler and Gertrude Enders Huntington, *Children
in Amish Society;* or Laurence W. Wylie (ed.), *Chanzeaux: A
Village in Anjou.*

Session 5: A Model for Religious Socialization.
Readings: C. Ellis Nelson, *Where Faith Begins.*

Session 6: Focus: Religion or Faith.
Readings: Wilfred Cantwell Smith, *The Meaning and End of Religion.*

Session 7: Mission: Cultural Continuity or Change.
Film: *Goodnight Socrates.*
Readings: H. Richard Niebuhr, *Christ and Culture;* Ivan Illich, *The Church, Change and Development;* Robert Nisbet, *The Social Bond;* or Julian H. Steward, *Theory of Culture Change.*

Session 8: Rites of Transition.
Film: *Bar Mitzvah.*
Readings: Victor W. Turner, *The Ritual Process,* or Arnold van Gennep, *Rites of Passage.*

Session 9: Rites of Intensification.
Readings: W. Lloyd Warner, *The Family of God;* or Raymond Panikkar, *Worship and Secular Man;* or Roy A. Rappaport, *Pigs for the Ancestors: Ritual in the Ecology of a New Guinea People.*

Session 10: The Social Construction of Reality.
Readings: Peter L. Berger and Thomas Luckmann, *The Social Construction of Reality;* Frederick Elkin and Gerald Handel, *The Child and Society;* or Jules Henry, *Culture Against Man.*

Session 11: Experience and Community.
Readings: Edward T. Hall, *The Hidden Dimension;* Conrad M. Arensberg and Solon T. Kimball, *Culture and Community;* or Evon Z. Vogt and Ethel Albert (eds.), *The People of Rimrock: A Study of Values in Five Cultures.*

Session 12: World Views and Life-Styles.
Film: *The Hutterites.*
Readings: Werner Jaeger, *Early Christianity and Greek Paideia;* Ian Muirhead, *Education in the New Testament;* Dorothy Lee, *Freedom and Culture;* Rosabeth M. Kanter, *Commitment and Community;* or Margaret Mead, *Coming of Age in Samoa.*

Session 13: Action for Liberation.

Readings: Paulo Freire, *Pedagogy of the Oppressed;* or Stanley Charnofsky, *Educating the Powerless;* or Edward A. Powers, *Signs of Shalom.*

Session 14: Religious Education: The Challenge.

Readings: John H. Westerhoff, *Values for Tomorrow's Children,* and Berard L. Marthaler, *Catechetics in Context.*

Requirements:

1. Regular attendance in class with active participation in small group activities. Class sessions are three hours and will combine lectures, group discussion, and other learning activities.

2. Readings and weekly book reports. Each session has one or more books listed which relate to the topic for consideration. You are to choose at least one of these books each week. You may want to assign books in small groups so as to get as much diversity as possible for discussion. After reading in your chosen book, you are to write a brief report to be used in class which answers the following questions: (a) What did you learn that was important to you? (b) What difference might this new knowledge or insight make in religious education?

3. An ethnographic study of an aspect of the church's life to be turned in at the end of the semester. The following books will aid you in the preparation of your study: Hortense Powdermaker, *Stranger and Friend;* James West, *Plainville USA;* Harry Wolcott, *A Kwakiutl Village and School;* James P. Spradley and David W. McCurdy, *The Cultural Experience;* Pierre Maranda, *Introduction to Anthropology.*

NOTES

Chapter 1: Protestants and Roman Catholics Together

1. *The Catechist* represents a forward-looking Roman Catholic magazine for religious educators. (Available from 38 W. Fifth St., Dayton, Ohio 45402.)

2. For the sake of our Protestant readers, The General Catechetical Directory is an official document of the Roman Catholic Church, an ecclesiastical "white paper" calling for a reappraisal and offering guidelines as to the nature, goals, means, content, structure, and organization of catechetical or educational activity in the Christian faith community. Its purpose is to guide in the production of catechetical directives and catechisms at the national and regional level. For further understanding and its history, see the introduction to *Catechetics in Context*.

3. Berard L. Marthaler, O.F.M. Conv., *Catechetics in Context* (Huntington, Ind.: Our Sunday Visitor, 1973). Combines the text of the General Catechetical Directory issued by the Sacred Congregation for the Clergy with notes and commentary by one of this country's most perceptive religious educators. It provides not only learned interpretation but creative insight into the nature, goals, means, content, structure, and organization of religious education for the Christian faith community.

4. The only other book that has equally captured my imagination is C. Ellis Nelson, *Where Faith Begins* (Richmond, Va.: John Knox Press, 1971). One of the most significant books on religious education written in this decade, it addresses the questions Why is there faith? and How is faith transmitted? Emphasizing that faith is communicated by a community of faith and that the meaning of faith is developed by its members out of their history, by their interaction with each other and in relation to the events that take place in their lives, Nelson provides both the professional and lay religious educator with a resource for rethinking the church's life and educational ministry.

5. C. Ellis Nelson, "A Protestant Response to the General Catechetical Directory," *The Living Light*, Vol. IX, No. 3 (Fall 1972), p. 93. Used by permission.

6. John H. Westerhoff III, *Values for Tomorrow's Children* (Philadelphia: United Church Press, 1970). Written as a tract for our times, a stimulus to the framing of an alternative future for education in the church.

7. John H. Westerhoff III (ed.), *A Colloquy on Christian Education* (Philadelphia: Pilgrim Press, 1972). A collection of essays on the present and future state of Christian education. See especially chapter 7, Toward a Definition of Christian Education, and chapter 9, A Socialization Model.

8. Walter Abbot, S.J. (ed.), *The Documents of Vatican II* (New York: Guild Press, 1966), p. 545.

9. W. J. Tobin (ed.), *International Catechetical Congress* (Washington: U.S. Catholic Conference, 1972), p. 4.

10. From *The General Catechetical Directory*, chapter One: Norms or Criteria. Section 45: Sources of Catechesis, quoted in Berard Marthaler, *Catechetics in Context*, p. 86.

184

11. For a thought-provoking article which addresses the issue of the nature of Christian education, see C. Ellis Nelson, "Is Christian Education Something Particular?" *Religious Education,* Vol. LXVII, No. 1 (Jan.–Feb. 1972), pp. 5–15. It is followed by a number of comments by religious educators from a wide variety of traditions.

12. Tobin (ed.), op. cit., p. 22.

13. Marthaler, op. cit., p. 51. Reprinted from *Catechetics in Context* by the permission of the publisher. © Copyright by Our Sunday Visitor, Inc., 1973.

14. Peter L. Berger and Thomas Luckmann, *The Social Construction of Reality* (Garden City, N.Y.: Doubleday, Anchor Books, 1967), p. 158. Used by permission.

Chapter 2: What Is Religious Socialization?

1. This chapter is adapted from an article, "A New Focus," which appeared in the November 1973 issue of the *Andover Newton Quarterly.* Used by permission.

2. Books on socialization abound. A few selected readings follow:

Philippe Aries, *Centuries of Childhood: A Social History of Family Life* (New York: Random House, 1962). A classic on the emergence of the concept of childhood as a distinctive period in the life cycle.

Orville G. Brim, Jr., and Stanton Wheeler, *Socialization After Childhood* (New York: John Wiley & Sons, 1966). Two essays which reflect on the often neglected subject of socialization after childhood.

John A. Clausen (ed.), *Socialization and Society* (Boston: Little, Brown and Co., 1968). An examination of socialization as used in several disciplines, cross-culturally, and at various phases of the life cycle.

Frederick Elkin and Gerald Handel, *The Child and Society,* 3rd ed. (New York: Random House, 1972). A short paperback text on the process of socialization. A good summary of up-to-date thought.

Erik H. Erikson, *Childhood and Society* (New York: W. W. Norton & Co., 1950). A classic treatment of stages of development and the relationship between childhood training and cultural characteristics. They are further developed in his work *Identity: Youth and Crisis* (New York: W. W. Norton & Co., 1968).

David A. Goslin (ed.), *A Handbook of Socialization Theory and Research* (Chicago: Rand McNally & Co., 1969). A mammoth (1,182-page) reference work containing twenty-nine articles summarizing all research in the field to date.

Kenneth Keniston, *Young Radicals: Notes on Committed Youth* (New York: Harcourt, Brace & World, 1968). Traces the development from childhood to young adulthood of a group of students sharing personal life histories intertwined with broader comments of history.

Philip Mayer, *Socialization: The Approach from Social Anthropology* (London: Tavistock, 1970).

Talcott Parsons, *Social Structure and Personality* (New York: Free Press of Glencoe, 1964). Examines various aspects of the social structure as they shape socialization.

Roberta S. Sigel (ed.), *Learning About Politics* (New York: Random House, 1970). A reader in political socialization, a topic of growing interest.

"Socialization and Schools," *Harvard Educational Review,* Reprint Series No. 1, 1968. Four articles on socialization as it occurs in educational institutions.

Melford E. Spiro, *Children of the Kibbutz: A Study in Child Training and Personality* (Cambridge, Mass.: Harvard University Press, 1958). Report of a fascinating social experiment.

Beatrice B. Whiting (ed.), *Six Cultures: Studies in Child-Rearing* (New York: John Wiley & Sons, 1963). Reports on research on child training and personality difference in Kenya, India, Okinawa, Mexico, New England (U.S.A.), and the Philippines.

John W. M. Whiting et al., *Field Guide for a Study of Socialization* (New York: John Wiley & Sons, 1966). An excellent introduction to the study of socialization.

Thomas Rhys Williams, *Introduction to Socialization: Human Culture Transmitted* (St. Louis: C. V. Mosby Co., 1972). A standard anthropology text in socialization.

3. Lawrence A. Cremin, *American Education: The Colonial Experience, 1607–1783* (New York: Harper & Row, 1971), p. xiii. Although it is a history of the early years of education in the United States, this is one of the most significant books I know on education from a broad cultural perspective. For an interview with Cremin on history, education, and culture, see "Freeing Ourselves from the Mythmakers" by John Westerhoff in *Perspectives on Education* (New York: Teachers College, Columbia University, Winter–Spring 1972), pp. 24–32.

4. Irvin L. Child, "Socialization," in Gardner Lindzey (ed.), *Handbook of Social Psychology*, Vol. II (New York: Addison Wesley, 1960), p. 655.

5. Understanding the nature of religion is difficult. The following books are recommended for those who would like to explore this phenomenon further:

Michael Banton (ed.), *Anthropological Approaches to the Study of Religion* (New York: Praeger Publishers, Inc., 1966).

Christopher Dawson, *Religion and Culture* (New York: Meridian Books, 1958). The Gifford Lectures of 1947 by a distinguished historian.

Jan De Vries, *The Study of Religion* (New York: Harcourt, Brace & World, 1968). A historical approach to understanding religion.

Annemarie De Waal Malefijt, *Religion and Culture* (New York: Macmillan, 1968). An excellent introduction to the anthropology of religion.

E. O. James, *The Social Function of Religion* (London: University of London Press, 1940). An old but still relevant comparative study of religion and society.

William James, *The Varieties of Religious Experience* (New York: Modern Library, 1902). A classic study in human nature and religion from a psychological point of view.

Gerardus Van Der Leeuw, *Religion in Essence and Development* (New York: Harper & Row, 1963). A pioneering classic in the phenomenology of religion.

William A. Lessa and Evon Z. Vogt (eds.), *Reader in Comparative Religion: An Anthropological Approach,* 3rd ed. (New York: Harper & Row, 1972). A series of original essays focusing on an anthropological approach to religion.

Louis Schneider (ed.), *Religion, Culture and Society* (New York: John Wiley & Sons, 1964). A reader in the sociology of religion.

Ninian Smart, *The Phenomenon of Religion* (New York: Herder & Herder, 1973). An exceptionally important book in the philosophy of religion by the author of *The Religious Experience of Mankind* (New York: Charles Scribner's Sons, 1969).

Wilfred Cantwell Smith, *The Meaning and End of Religion* (New York: Macmillan, 1962). A classic in our time—required reading for anyone concerned about the nature of religion.

Paul Tillich, *Dynamics of Faith* (New York: Harper & Brothers, 1957). An important theological work on religion and faith.

6. See James Fowler, "Faith Development: Theory and Research," Harvard Divinity School, Nov. 1972. An unpublished paper. Dr. Fowler has been building on the work of Lawrence Kohlberg in moral development and education, apply-

ing it to faith development and education. His work is original and its implications for religious education immense.

7. See Diana Lee Beach, "Sex Role Stereotyping in Church School Curricula" (Richmond, Va.: John Knox Press, 1972). This same subject is also explored in chapter 8, Sex and Socialization.

8. For a full treatment of this important issue, see Peter L. Berger and Thomas Luckmann, *The Social Construction of Reality* (Garden City, N.Y.: Doubleday, Anchor Books, 1967), pp. 158ff.

9. Joseph H. Fichter, S.J., "The Concept of Man in Social Science: Freedom, Values, and Second Nature," *Journal of the Scientific Study of Religion,* Vol. II, No. 2 (June 1972), pp. 110–21.

10. Peter L. Berger, *The Precarious Vision: An Essay on Social Perception and Christian Faith* (Garden City, N.Y.: Doubleday, 1961), p. 50.

11. I am very much aware of the work of B. F. Skinner and other behaviorists. In many ways I have been significantly influenced by their work. However, I find behaviorism, taken to its logical conclusions, scientifically and theologically untenable. For a discussion of Skinner's position, see: B. F. Skinner, *Science and Human Behavior* (New York: Macmillan, 1953), *Walden Two* (New York: Macmillan, 1963), *The Technology of Teaching* (New York: Appleton-Century-Crofts, 1968), *Verbal Behavior* (New York: Appleton-Century-Crofts, 1957), and *Beyond Freedom and Dignity* (New York: Macmillan, 1973).

12. Fichter, op. cit., p. 118.

Chapter 3: The Sacred Community—
Kin and Congregation in the Transmission of Culture

1. An earlier version of this article is to be published in the 1973 *Proceedings of the American Ethnological Society* (Seattle: University of Washington Press, in press).

2. These cultural areas and trends were first delineated by Arensberg in "Peoples of the World" in Conrad M. Arensberg and Solon T. Kimball, *Culture and Community* (New York: Harcourt, Brace & World, 1965). See also Charles H. Anderson, *White Protestant Americans* (Englewood Cliffs, N.J.: Prentice-Hall, 1970).

3. Milton M. Gordon, *Assimilation in American Life* (New York: Oxford University Press, 1964).

4. Victor W. Turner, *The Ritual Process* (Chicago: Aldine Publishing Co., 1969).

5. Arnold Van Gennep, *Rites of Passage* (Chicago: University of Chicago Press, 1960).

6. Gwen K. Neville, "Annual Assemblages as Related to the Persistence of Culture Patterns: An Anthropological Study of a Summer Community" (unpublished Ph.D. dissertation, University of Florida, 1971).

7. Eliot D. Chapple and Carleton Coon, *Principles of Anthropology* (New York: Holt, Rinehart & Winston, 1942).

8. Turner, op. cit. See his second section in which he discusses the sacredness of shared ritual experience, or *communitas.*

9. James G. Leyburn, *The Scotch-Irish, A Social History* (Chapel Hill, N.C.: University of North Carolina Press, 1962).

10. Ibid., p. 213.

11. K. L. Simpkins, "Folk fra Amerikas 13 Kolonier," in *Dansk Ethnologie* (Oct. 1973).

12. Robin Fox has discussed the concept of cognatic descent at length in his *Kinship and Marriage* (Baltimore: Penguin Books, 1967).

13. T. C. Smout, *A History of the Scottish People 1560–1830* (London: Wm. Collins & Sons, 1969).

14. Robert Burns's poem, "The Holy Fair," from *The Complete Poetical Works of Robert Burns*, Cambridge Edition (Boston: Houghton Mifflin Co., 1897), p. 11.

15. Thomas H. Spence, *The Presbyterian Congregation on Rocky River* (Kingsport, Tenn.: Kingsport Press, 1954), p. 168.

16. Archie Carr, *So Excellent a Fishe: A Natural History of Sea Turtles* (Garden City, N.Y.: Natural History Press, 1967).

17. W. Lloyd Warner, *The Family of God: A Symbolic Study of Christian Life in America* (New Haven, Conn.: Yale University Press, Yale Paperback, 1965).

18. Conrad M. Arensberg and Solon T. Kimball, *Culture and Community* (New York: Harcourt, Brace & World, 1965). See also: Joseph H. Fichter, *Dynamics of a City Church* (Chicago: University of Chicago Press, 1951), Rene König, *The Community* (New York: Schocken Books, 1968), and Rosabeth M. Kanter, *Commitment and Community* (Cambridge, Mass.: Harvard University Press, 1972).

Chapter 4: Religious Education
for the Maypole Dancers

1. "Religious Education for the Maypole Dancers" was first written and delivered in the fall of 1972 as the first of a series for the Lentz Lectures in Education in the Church at Harvard Divinity School. In that original form it was published in *Religious Education*, Vol. LXVIII (Sept.–Oct. 1973). (It has been rewritten for this book.) Reprinted (with revisions) from the September–October 1973 issue of *Religious Education* by permission of the publisher, The Religious Education Association, 409 Prospect St., New Haven, Conn. 06510.

2. Robert W. Lynn and Elliott Wright, *The Big Little School* (New York: Harper & Row, 1971), p. 98. This book on the history of the Sunday school movement in the United States is one of the most perceptive, creative works written in recent years. Its importance for both cultural history and planning the future of religious education is prodigious.

3. See Gwen K. Neville, "Annual Assemblages as Related to the Persistence of Cultural Patterns" (Ph.D. dissertation, University of Florida, 1971), University Microfilms.

4. See Charles H. Anderson, *White Protestant Americans* (Englewood Cliffs, N.J.: Prentice-Hall, 1970).

5. Milton M. Gordon, *Assimilation in American Life* (New York: Oxford University Press, 1964), p. 160.

6. Robert A. Nisbet, *Social Change and History* (New York: Oxford University Press, 1969), p. 271. See also Nisbet's *The Social Bond* (New York: Knopf, 1970) and chapter 10 of this book.

7. For a fascinating examination of "liberal main-line" and "conservative" churches, see Dean M. Kelley, *Why Conservative Churches Are Growing* (New York: Harper & Row, 1972). While Kelley provides us with an important study and analysis of the situation in churches today, I find his conclusions and implications misleading and unsatisfactory.

8. See James J. Gardiner and J. Deotis Roberts, *Quest for a Black Theology* (Philadelphia: United Church Press, 1971), and James H. Cone, *Black Theology and Black Power* (New York: Seabury Press, 1969).

9. For a particularly perceptive article on religious education, see Dwayne Huebner, "Education in the Church," *Andover Newton Quarterly*, Vol. 12, No. 3 (Jan. 1972).

10. A highly important chapter, entitled "Christian, Noun or Adjective," is found in Wilfred Cantwell Smith, *Questions of Religious Truth* (New York:

Charles Scribner's Sons, 1967). He makes the important distinction between asking, Are you *a* Christian? or, Are you Christian? He concludes that the latter, behavioral question, is the significant one for Christians. The implications of this essay for religious education are vast.

11. No other contemporary systematic theologian has been more important for my thinking than Harvard's Gordon Kaufman. For a thought-provoking discussion of world views, see Gordon D. Kaufman, "Secular, Religious, and Theistic World Views," in his *God: The Problem* (Cambridge, Mass.: Harvard University Press, 1972). Also see his *Systematic Theology: A Historicist Perspective* (New York: Charles Scribner's Sons, 1968).

12. I use the words intentional or purposeful socialization and religious education interchangeably. For another look at this threefold discussion of intentional socialization, see my chapter "A Socialization Model" in *A Colloquy on Christian Education* (Philadelphia: United Church Press, 1972).

13. My discussion of the Dakotas is taken from Dorothy Lee, "Responsibility Among the Dakota," in *Freedom and Culture* (New York: Prentice-Hall, Spectrum Books, 1959). I highly recommend all the essays in this book by one of our leading cultural anthropologists. Her discussion of freedom and autonomy within the confines of culture is profound.

14. James B. Pratt, *The Religious Consciousness* (New York: Macmillan, 1945), p. 97. This is an old but still relevant book for religious educators.

15. Soren Kierkegaard, *The Journal of Kierkegaard* (New York: Macmillan, 1958), p. 53.

16. See John D. Murray and Charles H. Anderson, *The Professors* (Cambridge, Mass.: Schenkmar Publishing Co., 1971).

17. See Peter L. Berger, *The Sacred Canopy* (Garden City, N.Y.: Doubleday, 1969).

18. See Andrew M. Greeley, *Religion in the Year 2000* (New York: Sheed & Ward, 1969); Peter L. Berger, *The Sacred Canopy* (Garden City, N.Y.: Doubleday, 1969); Robert N. Bellah, *Beyond Belief* (New York: Harper & Row, 1970); Thomas Luckmann, *The Invisible Religion* (New York: Macmillan, 1967); Clifford Geertz, "Religion as a Cultural System," in Donald R. Cutler (ed.), *The Religious Situation* (Boston: Beacon Press, 1968), pp. 639–87; Jurgen Habermas, *Toward a Rational Society* (Boston: Beacon Press, 1970); Gerhard Lenski, *The Religious Factor* (Garden City, N.Y.: Doubleday, 1963); and Martin E. Marty, *The Modern Schism* (New York: Harper & Row, 1969).

Chapter 5: Rites and Rituals for a Double World—
Private and Public Meanings

1. See Leach's definition of ritual in E. R. Leach, "Ritualization in Man in Relation to Conceptual and Social Development," in William Lessa and Evon Z. Vogt (eds.), *Reader in Comparative Religion*, 3rd ed. (New York: Harper & Row, 1972).

2. See Erving Goffman, *Interaction Ritual* (Chicago: Aldine Publishing Co., 1967). Also Edward T. Hall, *The Silent Language* (Garden City, N.Y.: Doubleday, 1966).

3. Leach, op. cit. See also Emile Durkheim, *Elementary Forms of the Religious Life* (New York: The Free Press of Glencoe, 1969; originally published 1915), and W. Lloyd Warner, *The Family of God* (New Haven, Conn.: Yale University Press, Yale Paperback, 1969).

4. Phillip Amerson, "Ritual and Community Life: A Study of the Koinonia Farms Community," unpublished paper presented as part of a seminar on An-

thropology of Religion, Emory University, 1973. Also see Dallas Lee, *The Cotton Patch Evidence* (New York: Harper & Row, 1971).

5. W. Lloyd Warner, *Black Civilization* (New York: Harper & Row, Harper Torchbooks, 1964).

6. E. Adamson Hoebel, *The Cheyennes: Warriors of the Great Plains* (New York: Holt, Rinehart & Winston, 1960).

7. See Eliot D. Chapple and Carleton Coon, *Principles of Anthropology* (New York: Holt, Rinehart & Winston, 1942).

8. Arnold Van Gennep, *Rites of Passage* (Chicago: University of Chicago Press, 1960; originally published in 1909).

9. See Raymond Panikkar, *Worship and Secular Man* (New York: Orbis Books, 1973). Other recommended books on worship from a theological-historical perspective are:

Louis Bouyer, *Liturgical Piety* (Notre Dame, Ind.: University of Notre Dame Press, 1947, and *Rite and Man: Natural Sacredness and Christian Liturgy* (Notre Dame, Ind.: University of Notre Dame Press, 1967). The first is a classic work on the nature of the Christian cult in the light of early history; the second is on the "human" character of Christian life and cultus.

Harvey Cox, *The Feast of Fools* (Cambridge: Harvard University Press, 1970). A contemporary examination of celebration.

J. G. Davies (ed.), *A Dictionary of Christian Worship and Liturgy* (New York: Macmillan, 1972). A helpful reference work.

Dom Gregory Dix, *The Shape of the Liturgy* (New York: Morehouse, 1945). Traces the historical development of Christian liturgy in the early church.

Mircea Eliade, *The Sacred and the Profane* (New York: Harcourt, Brace, 1947). A study of the significance of religion, myth, symbolism, and ritual within life and culture.

Willi Marxsen, *The Lord's Supper As a Christological Problem* (Philadelphia: Fortress Press, 1970). A significant and debatable book from the point of view of biblical exegesis.

William Nicholls, *Jacob's Ladder: The Meaning of Worship* (Richmond, Va.: John Knox Press, 1958). One of the most important of the Ecumenical Studies in Worship series.

James Shaughnessy (ed.), *The Roots of Ritual* (Grand Rapids: Eerdmans, 1973). The Murphy Center for Liturgical Research at Notre Dame looks at the question: Have modern persons outgrown their need for ritual?

James F. White, *New Forms of Worship* (Nashville: Abingdon Press, 1971). Emphasizes practice in the present.

One of the finest, most helpful, magazines I know is *Liturgy,* the journal of the Liturgical Conference, 1330 Massachusetts Avenue, N.W., Washington, D.C. 20005. I'd especially recommend the January 1973 issue (Vol. 18, No. 1), which includes the "New England Liturgical Week" lectures. Other books and resources from the Liturgical Conference are: Robert W. Hovda and Gabe Huck, *There's No Place Like People: Planning Small Group Liturgies;* Robert W. Hovda, *Dry Bones: Living Worship Guides to Good Liturgy;* Gabe Huck and Virginia Sloyan, *Parishes and Families;* and Virginia Sloyan and Gabe Huck, *Children's Liturgies.* Also to be recommended is the *Celebration Packet* (which includes a book "Toward Celebration," a liturgical simulation exercise, and a recording "Celebration Sharings and Sounds"), published by United Church Press, 1505 Race Street, Philadelphia, Pa. 19102.

10. Harvey Cox's *The Seduction of the Spirit* (New York: Simon and Schuster, 1973) provides another significant resource for understanding the role and importance of liturgies and celebrations. Especially in chapter 6, where he

describes an unusual Easter Mass, new dimensions of celebration are provided.

Chapter 6: The Faith of Children

1. See John Hostetler and Gertrude Enders Huntington, *Children in Amish Society* (New York: Holt, Rinehart & Winston, 1971). This is an excellent example of an ethnographic study of socialization and community education. It is one of a number of recommended studies in education and culture.

2. The following case studies of four children are based upon material contained in Ann Trevelyan's report, "A Study of Four Children and Their Faith and Religion" (Jan. 15, 1973), presented in partial fulfillment for the course "The Church As a Learning Community" at Harvard Divinity School in the fall of 1972. I would like to acknowledge appreciation for her excellent piece of work. The names of people and places have, in some cases, been changed to protect the privacy of the children involved.

Chapter 7: The Learning of Values

1. Louis Raths et al., *Values and Teaching* (revised edition; Columbus, Ohio: Charles Merrill, 1966).

2. A number of excellent books on values clarification exists. They include: Sidney Simon et al., *Values Clarification* (New York: Hart, 1972); Merrill Harmin et al., *Clarifying Values Through Subject Matter* (Minneapolis: Winston Press, 1973). The best educational resource available on values clarification is an educational packet, "An Introduction to Value Education," prepared by the Educational and Consumer Relations Department of J. C. Penney Company, 1301 Avenue of the Americas, New York, N.Y. 10019. A continuing resource is the *Humanistic Education Quarterly*, edited by Howard Kirschenbaum, c/o AMHEC, Upper Jay, N.Y. 12987.

3. Evon Z. Vogt and Ethel Albert (eds.), *People of Rimrock* (Cambridge, Mass.: Harvard University Press, 1966).

4. John Whiting et al., "The Learning of Values," in Vogt and Albert (eds.), *People of Rimrock*, p. 115.

5. During the 1940s and early 1950s a very popular tradition of anthropological research was in a field called "culture and personality studies." These have been widely referred to in the literature of both social psychology and education. Some examples of this research tradition are: John William Whiting and Irvin L. Child, *Child-Training and Personality* (New Haven: Yale University Press, 1953); Dorothy Lee, *Freedom and Culture* (New York: Prentice-Hall, Spectrum Books, 1959); Dorothea Leighton and Clyde Kluckhohn, *The Children of the People* (Cambridge, Mass.: Harvard University Press, 1948); Margaret Mead, *Growing Up in New Guinea* (London: G. Ranoledge & Sons, 1931), and *Coming of Age in Samoa* (New York: William Morrow & Co., 1928).

Chapter 8: Sex and Socialization

1. Adapted from "Religious Socialization of Women in U.S. Subcultures" by Gwen Kennedy Neville, published in *Sexist Religion and Women in the Churches: No More Silence*, ed. Alice Hageman, copyright 1974. Used by permission of Association Press.

2. Lenore J. Weinstein et al., "Sex-Role Socialization in Picture Books for Preschool Children," *American Journal of Sociology*, Vol. 77, No. 6, pp. 1125–51. Also see Diana Lee Beach, "Sex Role Stereotyping in Church School Curricula" (Richmond, Va.: John Knox Press, 1972).

3. Charles H. Anderson, *White Protestant Americans* (Englewood Cliffs, N.J.: Prentice-Hall, 1970).

4. W. Lloyd Warner, *The Family of God* (New Haven: Yale University Press, Yale Paperback, 1969).

5. Dan Greenburg, *How to Be a Jewish Mother* (New York: Trident Press, 1964).

6. See chapter 4.

7. Monroe Lefkowitz et al., "Environmental Variable as Predictors of Aggressive Behavior," an unpublished paper presented at the annual meeting of the American Association for the Advancement of Science, Washington, D.C., December 29, 1972.

8. Emily C. Hewitt and Suzanne R. Hiatt, *Women Priests, Yes or No?* (New York: Seabury Press, 1973); Krister Stendahl, *The Bible and the Role of Women: A Case Study in Hermeneutics,* translated by Emilie T. Sander (Philadelphia: Fortress Press, 1966). Other helpful books are: Elsie Thomas Culver, *Women in the World of Religion* (Garden City, N.Y.: Doubleday, 1967); Mary Daly, *The Church and the Second Sex* (New York: Harper & Row, 1968); Sarah Bentley Doley (ed.), *Women's Liberation and the Church* (New York: Association Press, 1970); and Margaret Sittler Ermarth, *Adam's Fractured Rib* (Philadelphia: Fortress Press, 1970).

Chapter 9: Reshaping Adults

1. See Orville G. Brim, Jr., and Stanton Wheeler, *Socialization After Childhood* (New York: John Wiley & Sons, 1966).

2. Seymour Sarason, *The Culture of the School and the Problem of Change* (Rockleigh, N.J.: Allyn & Bacon, 1971).

3. For a positive look at evangelism and education from a perspective close to my own, see Gabriel Fackre, *Do and Tell: Engagement Evangelism in the Seventies* (Grand Rapids, Mich.: Eerdmans, 1973).

4. See *Colloquy* (Dec. 1972), which focuses on education and evangelism.

5. The Shalom Curriculum is a new educational program for churches, developed by the United Church of Christ especially for use in the Joint Educational Development (JED) denominations: Episcopal Church, United Church of Christ, United Presbyterian Church in the U.S.A., Disciples of Christ, Presbyterian Church in the U.S., and Reformed Church in America.

6. Edward A. Powers, *Signs of Shalom* (Philadelphia: United Church Press, 1973), is one of the most important books on Christian education published in the last few years. Within its pages will be found: insights into the biblical concept of shalom; suggestions for what an affirmation of their goal might imply for the life of particular congregations; planning aids to help local churches develop educational programs consistent with shalom; and finally, information on the variety of resources available to aid churches in the actualization of their plans.

7. See Lawrence Kohlberg, "Development As the Aim of Education," *Harvard Educational Review,* Vol. 42 (Nov. 1972), and Lawrence Kohlberg, "Education for Justice," in Theodore Sizer (ed.), *Moral Education* (Cambridge, Mass.: Harvard University Press, 1972).

8. *Colloquy* magazine (published by the United Church Press, 1505 Race Street, Philadelphia, Pa. 19102), since its first issue in January 1968, has been committed to helping educators rethink the church's educational mission and ministry in light of the concerns expressed in this chapter.

Chapter 10: Continuity and Change in Human Culture

1. This article originally appeared in the September 1972 issue of *Colloquy* under the title "Human Beings and Social Change." Used by permission.

2. Robert A. Nisbet, *Social Change and History* (New York: Oxford University Press, 1969).

3. Lynn Meloy, "Controversy as a New Catalyst in Christian Education," unpublished paper in partial fulfillment of a Harvard Divinity School course, "The Church as a Learning Community," January 18, 1973.

4. See Christopher Dawson, *Religion and Culture* (New York: Meridian Books, 1958), p. 206.

5. To close this book, I'd like to list a number of books on education which have not been quoted but which have influenced my thinking:

Wilbur Brookover and Edsel Ericson, *Society, School and Learning* (Rockleigh, N.J.: Allyn & Bacon, 1969).

Joseph Featherstone, *Schools Where Children Learn* (New York: Liveright, 1971).

Paulo Freire, *Education for Critical Consciousness* (New York: Seabury Press, 1973), and *Pedagogy for the Oppressed* (New York: Herder & Herder, 1971).

Thomas F. Green, *The Activities of Teaching* (New York: McGraw-Hill, 1971).

Harvard Educational Review. Cambridge: Harvard Graduate School of Education.

Francis K. Hsu (ed.), *Kinship and Culture* (Chicago: Aldine, 1971).

Ronald T. Hyman (ed.), *Approaches in Curriculum* (Englewood Cliffs, N.J.: Prentice-Hall, 1973).

Francis A. Ianni, *Culture, System and Behavior* (Chicago: Science Research Associates, 1967).

Bruce Joyce and Marsha Weil, *Models of Teaching* (Englewood Cliffs, N.J.: Prentice-Hall, 1972).

Jerome Kagan, *Understanding Children* (New York: Harcourt Brace Jovanovich, 1971).

Solon T. Kimball and James E. McClellan, *Education and the New America* (New York: Random House, 1962).

George Kneller, *Educational Anthropology* (New York: John Wiley & Sons, 1965).

Gerald S. Lesser (ed.), *Psychology and Educational Practice* (Glenview, Ill.: Scott, Foresman & Co., 1971).

Harry Lindquist (ed.), *Education* (Boston: Houghton Mifflin Co., 1970).

John Middleton (ed.), *From Child to Adult* (New York: Natural History Press, 1970).

Patricia Minuchin et al., *The Psychological Impact of School Experience* (New York: Basic Books, 1969).

Clara Nicholson, *Anthropology and Education* (Columbus, Ohio: Charles E. Merrill Books, 1968).

Philip H. Phenix, *Realms of Meaning* (New York: McGraw-Hill, 1964).

Jean Piaget, *Six Psychological Studies* (New York: Random House, 1967).

Mary Ann Pulaski, *Understanding Piaget* (New York: Harper & Row, 1971).

George D. Spindler, *Education and Culture* (New York: Holt, Rinehart & Winston, 1963).

David B. Tyack (ed.), *Turning Points in American Educational History* (Waltham, Mass.: Blaisdell Publishing Co., 1967).

Murray L. Wax et al. (eds.), *Anthropological Perspectives on Education* (New York: Basic Books, 1971).

Burton White and Jean Watts, *Experience and Environment* (Englewood Cliffs, N.J.: Prentice-Hall, 1973).